Dinah Zike's
Reading and Study Skills

McGraw Hill **Glencoe**

New York, New York   Columbus, Ohio   Chicago, Illinois   Peoria, Illinois   Woodland Hills, California

Glencoe/McGraw-Hill

A Division of The McGraw·Hill Companies

Send all inquiries to:
Glencoe/McGraw-Hill
8787 Orion Place
Columbus, OH 43240-4027

ISBN 0-07-845181-7

Printed in the United States of America

3 4 5 6 7 8 9 10   079   08 07 06 05 04

Table of Contents

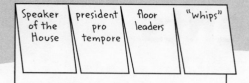

Chapter-Specific Foldables 49

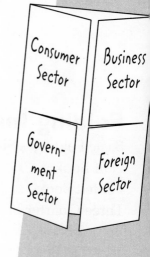

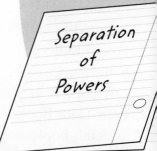

Dear Teacher,

What is a Foldable?

A Foldable is a 3-D, student-made, interactive graphic organizer based upon a skill. Making a Foldable gives students a fast, kinesthetic activity that helps them organize and retain information. Every chapter in the student edition of the textbook begins with a Foldable that is used as a Study Organizer. Each chapter's Foldable is designed to be used as a study guide for the main ideas and key points presented in sections of the chapter. Foldables can also be used for a more in-depth investigation of a concept, idea, opinion, event, or a person or place studied in a chapter. The purpose of this ancillary is to show you how to create various types of Foldables and provide chapter-specific Foldables examples. With this information, you can individualize Foldables to meet your curriculum needs.

This book is divided into two sections. The first section presents step-by-step instructions, illustrations, and photographs of 34 Foldables, many of which were not used in the student edition. I've included over 100 photographs to help you visualize ways in which they might enhance instruction. The second section presents two extra ideas on how to use Foldables for each chapter in the textbook. You can use the instruction section to design your own Foldables or alter the Foldables presented in each chapter as well. I highly suggest making this book available as a source for students who wish to learn new and creative ways in which to make study guides, present projects, or do extra credit work.

Who Am I?

You may have seen Foldables featured in this book used in supplemental programs or staff-development workshops. Today my Foldables are used internationally. I present workshops and keynotes to over fifty thousand teachers and parents a year, sharing Foldables that I began inventing, designing, and adapting over thirty five years ago. Students of all ages are using them for daily work, note-taking activities, student-directed projects, forms of alternative assessment, journals, graphs, tables, and more.

Have fun using and adapting Foldables,

Dinah Zike

Why use Foldables in Social Studies?

When teachers ask me why they should take time to use the Foldables featured in this book, I explain that they:

. . . organize, display, and arrange information, making it easier for students to grasp social studies concepts, theories, facts, opinions, questions, research, and ideas.

. . . are student-made study guides that are compiled as students listen for main ideas, read for main ideas, or conduct research.

. . . provide a multitude of creative formats in which students can present projects, research, interviews, and inquiry-based reports.

. . . replace teacher-generated writing or photocopied sheets with student-generated print.

. . . incorporate the use of such skills as comparing and contrasting, recognizing cause and effect, and finding similarities and differences.

. . . continue to "immerse" students in previously learned vocabulary, concepts, information, generalizations, ideas, and theories, providing them with a strong foundation that they can build upon with new observations, concepts, and knowledge.

. . . can be used by students or teachers to easily communicate data through graphs, tables, charts, models, and diagrams, including Venn diagrams.

. . . allow students to make their own journals for recording observations, research information, primary and secondary source data, surveys, and so on.

. . . can be used as alternative assessment tools by teachers to evaluate student progress or by students to evaluate their own progress.

. . . integrate language arts, the sciences, and mathematics into the study of social studies.

. . . provide a sense of student ownership or investiture in the social studies curriculum.

Foldables and the NCSS Thematic Strands

In *Curriculum Standards for Social Studies: Expectations of Excellence,* the National Council for the Social Studies (NCSS) identified 10 themes that serve as organizing strands for the social studies curriculum at every school level. The themes include:

I. Culture
II. Time, Continuity, and Change
III. People, Places, and Environments
IV. Individual Development and Identity
V. Individuals, Groups, and Institutions
VI. Power, Authority, and Governance
VII. Production, Distribution, and Consumption
VIII. Science, Technology, and Society
IX. Global Connections
X. Civic Ideals and Practices

Students are expected to master specific skills that are organized around these themes, such as analyzing data, comparing and contrasting similarities and differences, explaining and describing concepts, and identifying cause-and-effect relationships.

Foldables help students practice and master these specific skills. Foldables require students to identify and describe main ideas, relationships, and processes. In most cases, students need to understand and comprehend information before they can illustrate it in a foldable. Foldables help students think, analyze, and communicate.

Foldable Basics

What to Write and Where

Teach students to write general information such as titles, vocabulary words, concepts, questions, main ideas, and dates on the front tabs of their Foldables. This way students can easily recognize main ideas and important concepts. Foldables help students focus on and remember key points without being distracted by other print.

Ask students to write specific information such as supporting ideas, student thoughts, answers to questions, research information, class notes, observations, and definitions under the tabs.

As you teach, demonstrate different ways in which Foldables can be used. Soon you will find that students make their own Foldables and use them independently for study guides and projects.

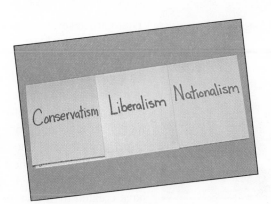

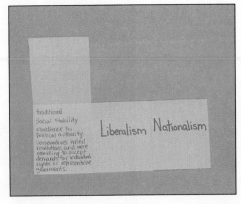

With or Without Tabs

Foldables with flaps or tabs create study guides that students can use to check what they know about the general information on the front of tabs. Use Foldables without tabs for assessment purposes or projects where information is presented for others to view quickly.

Venn diagram used as a study guide

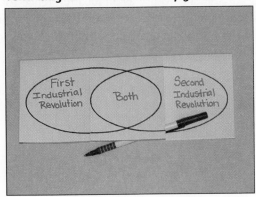

Venn diagram used for assessment

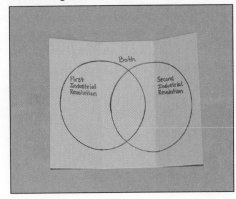

What to Do With Scissors and Glue

If it is difficult for your students to keep glue and scissors at their desks, set up a small table in the classroom and provide several containers of glue, numerous pairs of scissors (sometimes tied to the table), containers of crayons and colored pencils, a stapler, clear tape, and anything else you think students might need to make their Foldables.

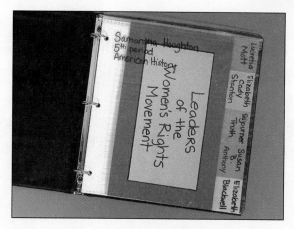

Storing Foldables

There are several ways that students can store their Foldables. They can use grocery bags, plastic bags, or shoeboxes. Students can also punch holes in their Foldables and place them in a three-ring binder. Suggest they place strips of two-inch clear tape along one side and punch three holes through the taped edge.

By keeping all of their Foldables together and organized, students will have created their own portfolio.

HINT: *I found it more convenient to keep student portfolios in my classroom so student work was always available when needed. Giant detergent boxes make good storage containers for portfolios.*

Use This Book as a Creative Resource

Have this book readily available for students to use as an idea reference for projects, discussions, social studies debates, extra credit work, cooperative learning group presentations, and so on. Encourage students to think of their own versions of Foldables to help them learn the material the best way possible.

Using Visuals and Graphics With Foldables

The graphics on pages 6–12 can be used as visual aids for students' Foldables. Students can incorporate them into their journals, notes, projects, and study guides independently. I found that students and teachers were more likely to use graphics if they were available on a classroom computer where they could be selected and printed out as needed. You can also photocopy and distribute the pages that follow for students to trace or cut out for their projects. All these visuals will aid student understanding and retention.

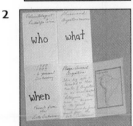

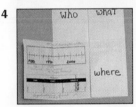

1. Students can mark and label large United States and world maps to show where past and recent events occurred, where a historic person lived and worked, where wars were fought and battles won, where volcanoes are active and inactive, where boundaries of territories or regions existed, and so on.

2. Students can mark and label smaller maps of continents to illustrate more specific locations. For example, when making a *who, what, when, where* Foldable, students can identify exactly where the particular event occurred or where the individual lived.

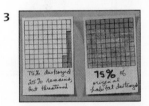

3. Bar graphs, grids, and circle graphs can be used to show changes over time, population distribution, and so on.

4. Use time lines to record when someone lived or when an event or sequence of events occurred. Use two time lines to compare what was happening in two different areas at the same time.

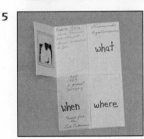

5. Use small picture frames to sketch or name a person, place, or thing.

Africa

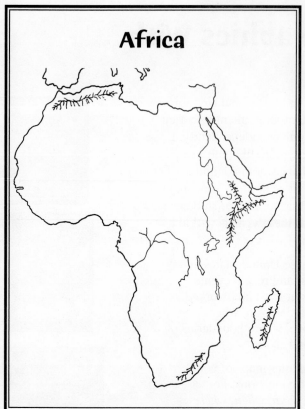

Antarctica

Asia

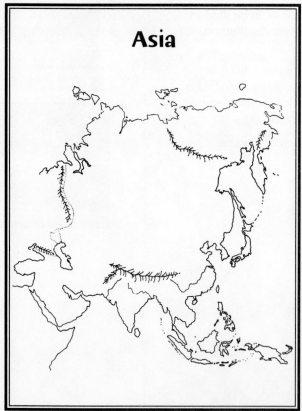

Australia

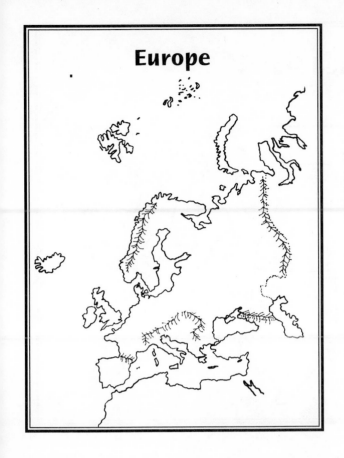

Europe

North America

South America

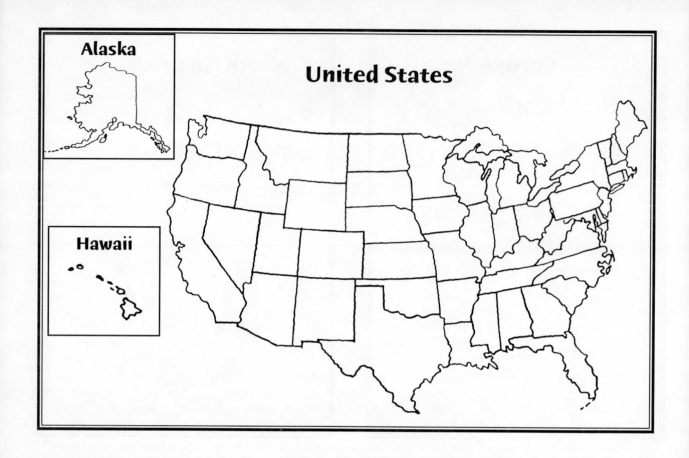

Alaska

Hawaii

United States

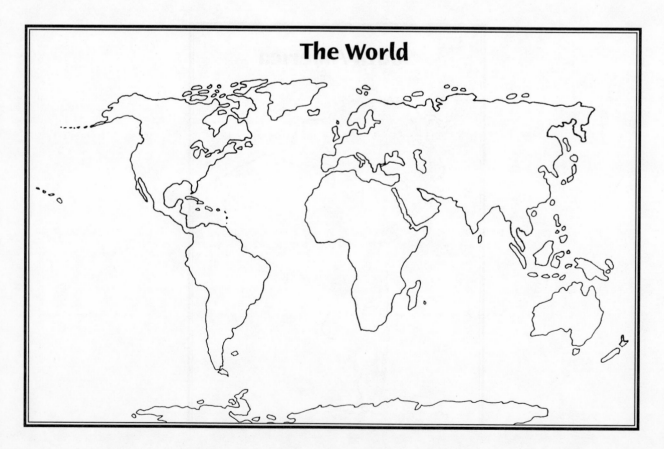

The World

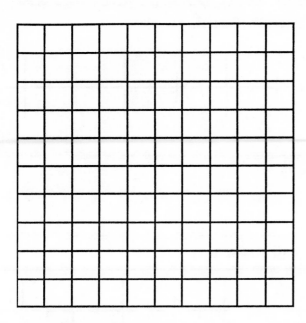

Percentages or bar graph

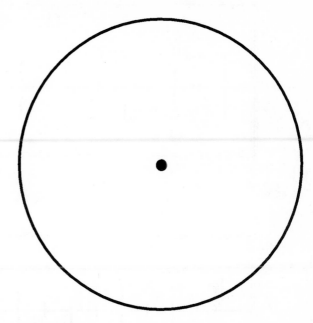

Circle graph

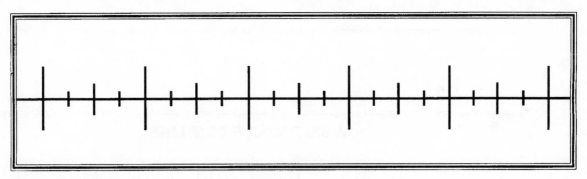

Generic Time Line

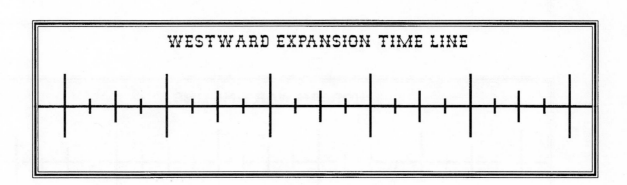

WESTWARD EXPANSION TIME LINE

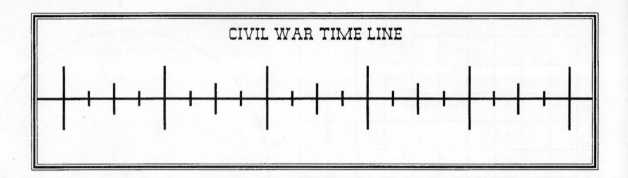

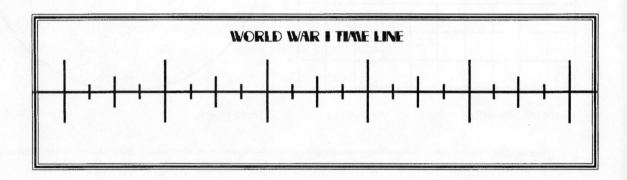

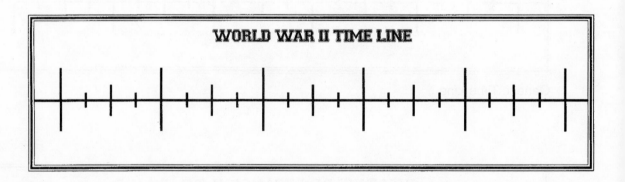

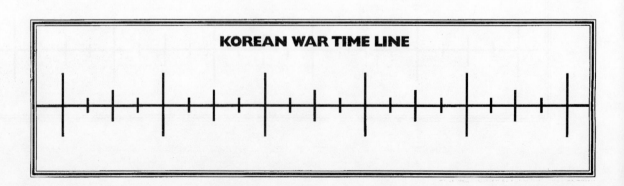

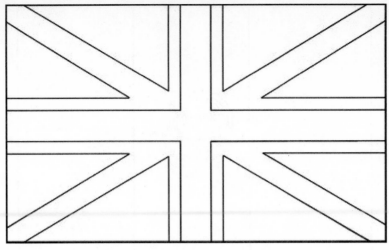

England

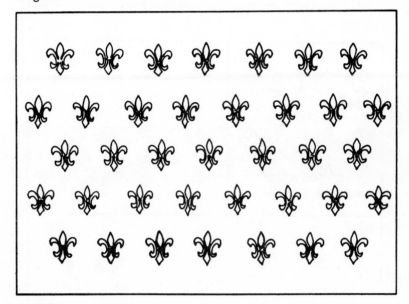

France

Spain

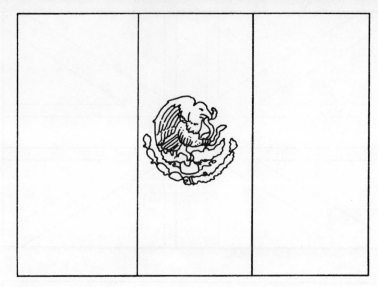

Mexico

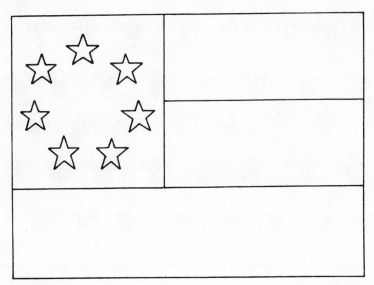

Confederacy

United States of America

Basic Foldables Shapes

The following figures illustrate the basic folds that are referred to throughout the instruction section of this book.

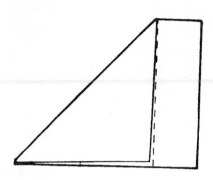

Taco Fold

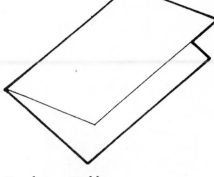

Hamburger Fold

Hot Dog Fold

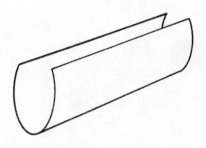

Burrito Fold

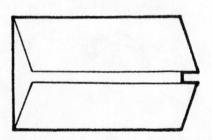

Shutter Fold

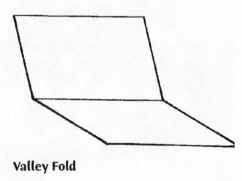

Valley Fold

Mountain Fold

Half Book

Fold a sheet of paper in half.

1. This book can be folded vertically like a *hot dog* or . . .

2. . . . it can be folded horizontally like a *hamburger.*

Use this book for descriptive, expository, persuasive, or narrative writing, as well as graphs, diagrams, or charts.

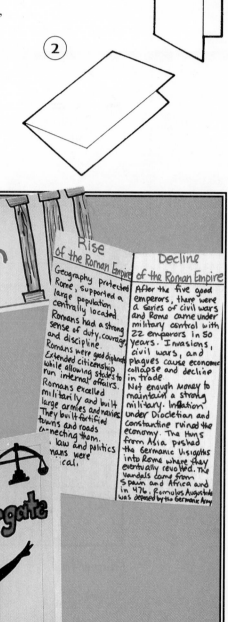

Nelson Mandela

APARTHEID

The Roman Empire

Rise
of the Roman Empire

Geography protected Rome, supported a large population centrally located.
Romans had a strong sense of duty, courage, and discipline.
Romans were good diplomats. Extended citizenship while allowing states to run internal affairs.
Romans excelled militarily and built large armies and navies. They built fortified towns and roads connecting them.
... law and politics ...mans were ...ical.

Decline
of the Roman Empire

After the five good emperors, there were a series of civil wars and Rome came under military control with 22 emperors in 50 years. Invasions, civil wars, and plagues cause economic collapse and decline in trade.
Not enough money to maintain a strong military. Inflation under Diocletian and Constantine ruined the economy. The Huns from Asia pushed the Germanic Visigoths into Rome where they eventually revolted. The Vandals came from Spain and Africa and in 476, Romulus Augustulus was deposed by the Germanic Army

The Seven Continents

1519

1821

Spain in Texas

Watergate

Folded Book

1. Make a *half-book*. (p. 14)

2. Fold it in half again like a *hamburger*. This makes a ready-made cover and two small pages for information on the inside.

Use photocopied work sheets, Internet printouts, and student-drawn diagrams or maps to make this book. One sheet of paper becomes two activities and two grades.

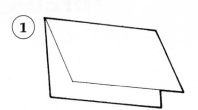

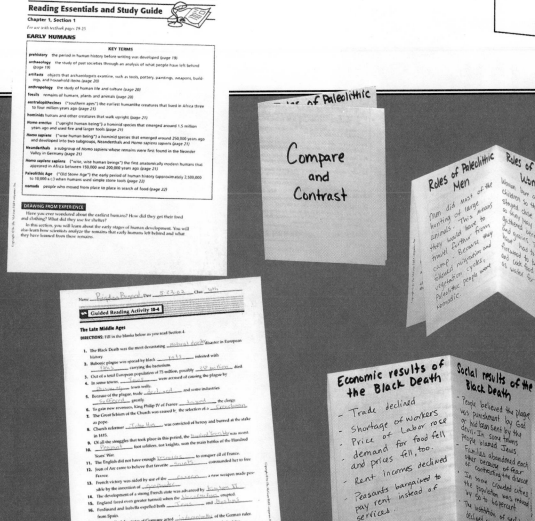

When folded, the worksheet becomes a book for recording notes and questions.

Three-Quarter Book

1. Make a *two-tab book* (p. 18) and raise the left-hand tab.

2. Cut the tab off at the top fold line.

3. A larger book of information can be made by gluing several *three-quarter books* side by side.

Sketch or glue a graphic to the left, write one or more questions on the right, and record answers and information under the right tab.

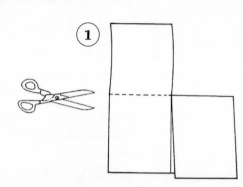

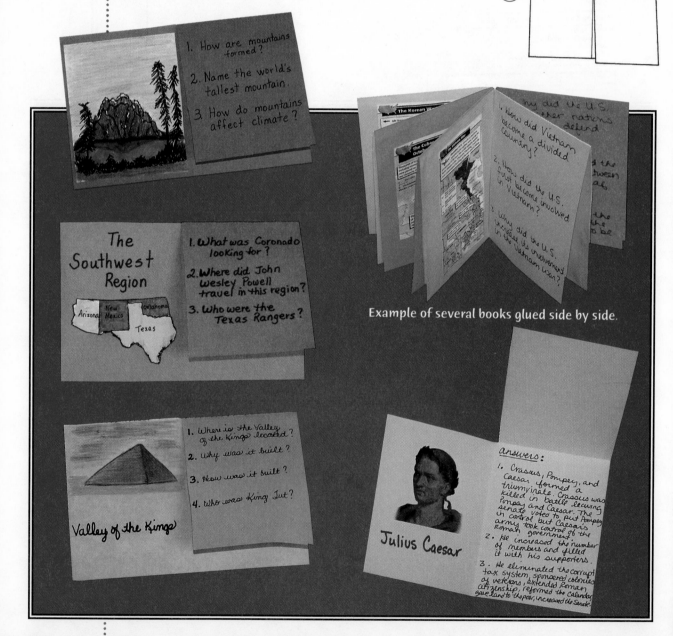

Example of several books glued side by side.

Bound Book

1. Take two sheets of paper and fold them separately like a *hamburger*. Place the papers on top of each other, leaving one-sixteenth of an inch between the *mountain tops*.

2. Mark both folds one inch from the outer edges.

3. On one of the folded sheets, cut slits in the middle to the marked spot on both sides.

4. On the second folded sheet, start at one of the marked spots and cut the fold between the two marks.

5. Take the cut sheet from step 3 and fold it like a *burrito*. Place the *burrito* through the other sheet and then open the *burrito*. Fold the bound pages in half to form an eight-page book.

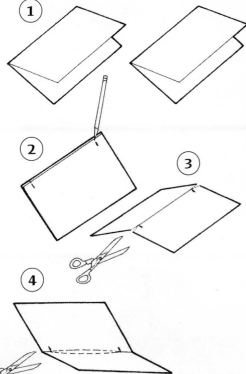

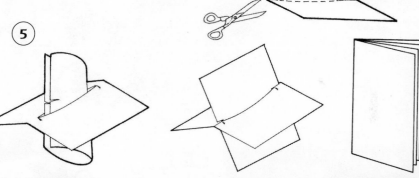

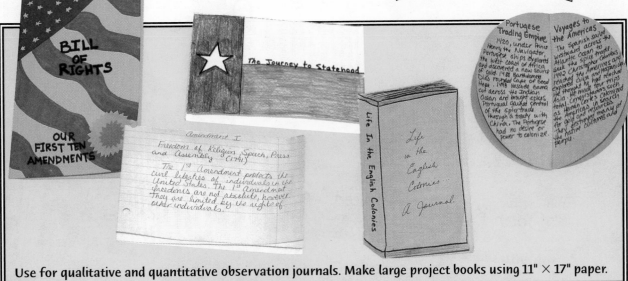

Use for qualitative and quantitative observation journals. Make large project books using 11" × 17" paper.

Two-Tab Book

1. Make a *folded book* (p. 15) and cut up the *valley* of the inside fold toward the *mountain top*. This cut forms two large tabs that can be used for text and illustrations on the front and back.

2. The book can be expanded by making several of these folds and gluing them side by side.

Use this book for learning about two things. For example, use it for comparing and contrasting, determining cause and effect, finding similarities and differences, using Venn diagrams, and so on.

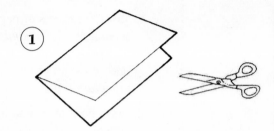

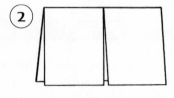

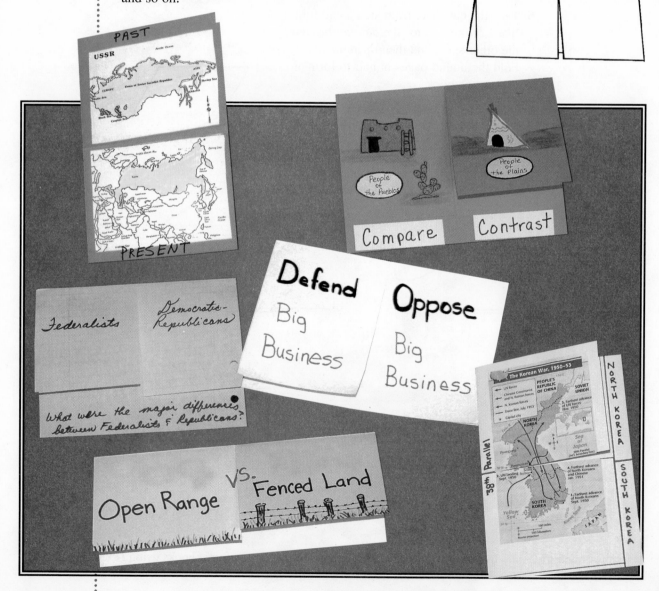

Pocket Book

1. Fold a sheet of paper in half like a *hamburger.*

2. Open the folded paper and fold one of the long sides up two inches to form a pocket. Refold along the *hamburger* fold so that the newly formed pockets are on the inside.

3. Glue the outer edges of the two-inch fold with a small amount of glue.

4. **Optional:** Glue a cover around the *pocket book.*

   Variation: Make a multi-paged booklet by gluing several pockets side by side. Glue a cover around the multi-paged *pocket book.*

Summarize information on note cards or on quarter sheets of notebook paper. Store other foldables, such as *two-tab books,* inside the pockets.

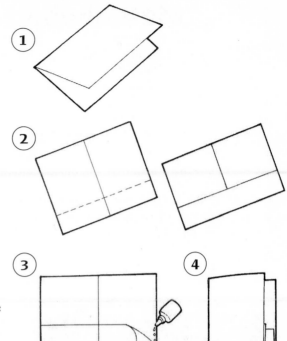

Matchbook

1. Fold a sheet of paper like a *hamburger,* but fold it so that one side is one inch longer than the other side.

2. Fold the one-inch tab over the short side forming a fold like an envelope.

3. Cut the front flap in half toward the *mountain top* to create two flaps.

Use this book to report on one thing, such as a person, place, or thing, or for reporting on two things, such as the cause and effect of Western Expansion.

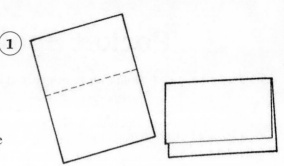

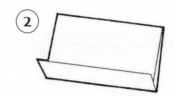

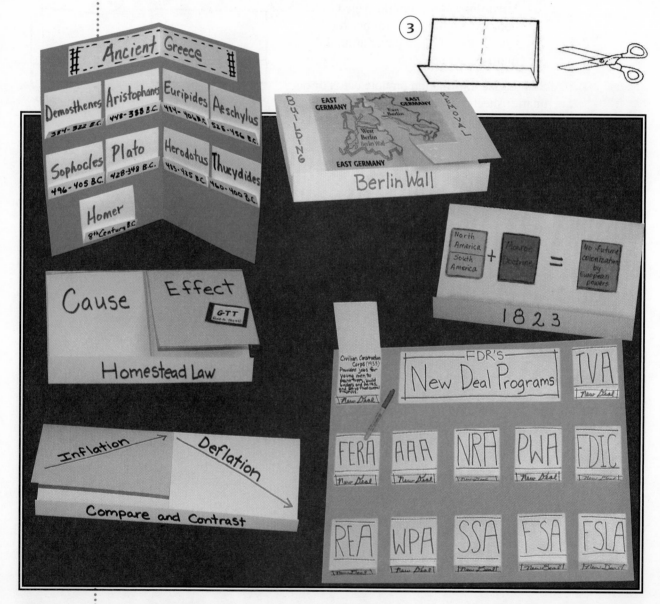

Shutter Fold

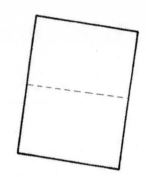

1. Begin as if you were going to make a *hamburger* but instead of creasing the paper, pinch it to show the midpoint.

2. Fold the outer edges of the paper to meet at the pinch, or mid-point, forming a *shutter fold*.

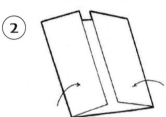

Use this book for comparing two things. Students could also make this foldable with 11" × 17" paper and then glue smaller books—such as the *half book, journal,* and *two-tab book*—inside to create a large project full of student work.

Trifold Book

1. Fold a sheet of paper into thirds.

2. Use this book as is, or cut into shapes. If the trifold is cut, leave plenty of paper on both sides of the designed shape, so the book will open and close in three sections.

Use this book to make charts with three columns or rows, large Venn diagrams, reports on three events or people, or to show and explain the outside and inside of something.

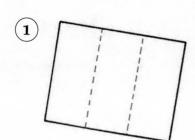

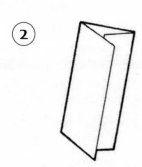

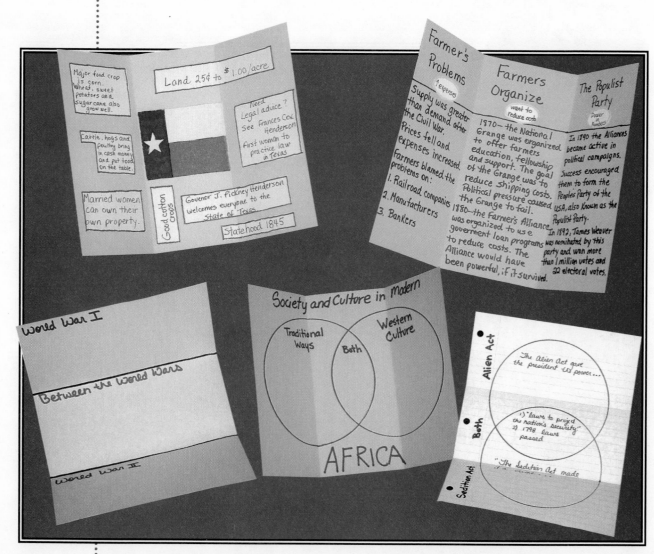

Three-Tab Book

1. Fold a sheet of paper like a *hot dog*.

2. With the paper horizontal, and the fold of the *hot dog* up, fold the right side toward the center, trying to cover one-third of the paper.

   NOTE: *If you fold the right edge over first, the final foldable will open and close like a book.*

3. Fold the left side over the right side to make a book with three folds.

4. Open the folded book. Place your hands between the two thicknesses of paper and cut up the two *valleys* on the top layer only along both folds. This will make three tabs.

Use this book for writing information about three things and for Venn diagrams.

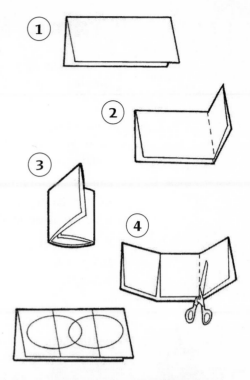

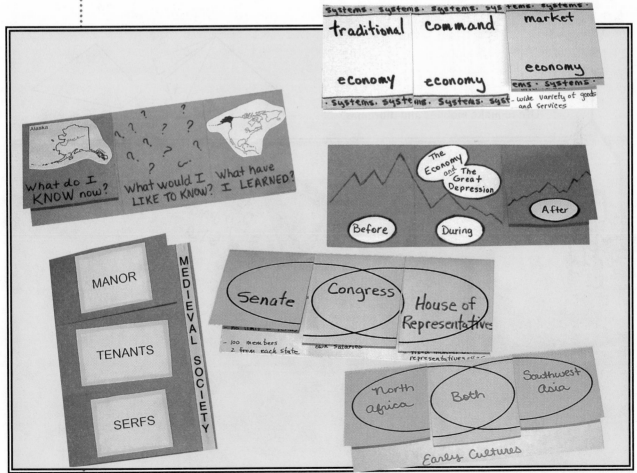

Pyramid Fold

1. Fold a sheet of paper into a *taco*, forming a square. Cut off the leftover piece.

2. Fold the triangle in half. Unfold. The folds will form an X dividing four equal sections.

3. Cut up one fold line and stop at the middle. Draw an X on one tab and label the other three.

4. Fold the X flap under the other flap and glue together. This makes a three-sided pyramid.

Label front sections and write information, notes, thoughts, and questions inside the pyramid on the back of the appropriate tab.

Use to make mobiles and dioramas.

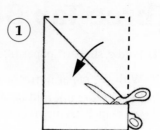

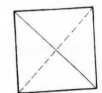

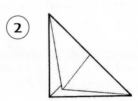

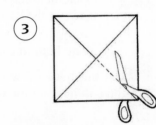

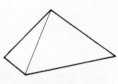

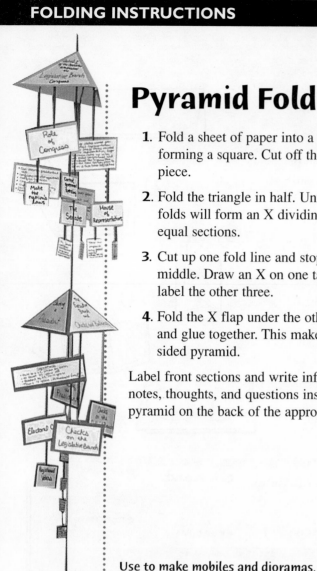

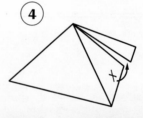

Record data inside the pyramid.

Glue four pyramids together to form a diorama showing four parts or stages.

Layered-Look Book

1. Stack two sheets of paper so that the back sheet is one inch higher than the front sheet.

2. Fold up the bottom edges of the paper to form four tabs. Align the edges so that all of the layers or tabs are the same distance apart.

3. When all tabs are the same size, crease the paper to hold the tabs in place and staple or glue the sheets together.

Glue the sheets together along the *valley* or inner center fold or staple them along the *mountain top*.

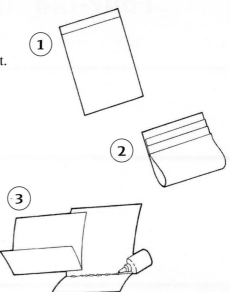

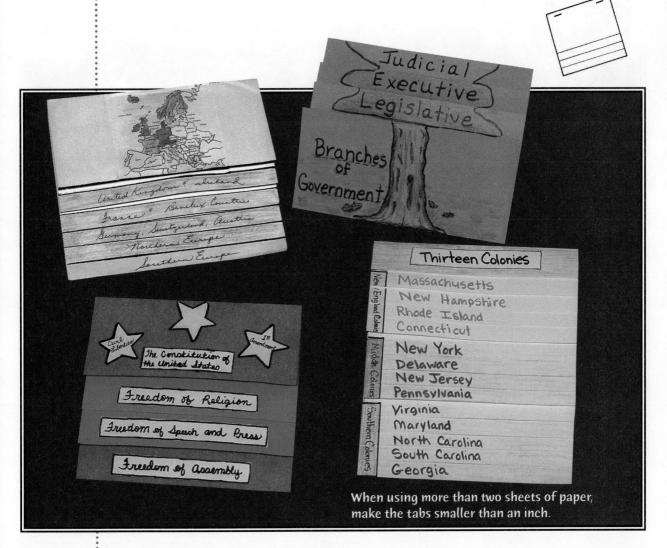

When using more than two sheets of paper, make the tabs smaller than an inch.

Four-Tab Book

1. Fold a sheet of paper in half like a *hot dog*.

2. Fold this long rectangle in half like a *hamburger*.

3. Fold both ends back to touch the *mountain top*.

4. On the side with two *valleys* and one *mountain top*, cut along the three inside fold lines on the front flap to make four tabs.

Use this book for recording information on four things, events, or people.

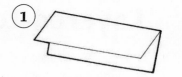

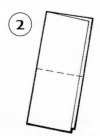

Standing Cube

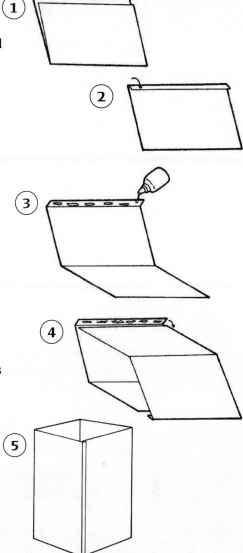

1. Use two sheets of the same size paper. Fold each like a *hamburger.* However, fold one side one-half inch shorter than the other side. This will make a tab that extends out one-half inch on one side.

2. Fold the long side over the short side of both sheets of paper, making tabs.

3. On one of the folded papers, place a small amount of glue along the the small folded tab next to the *valley,* but not in it.

4. Place the non-folded edge of the second sheet of paper square into the *valley* and fold the glue-covered tab over this sheet of paper. Press flat until the glue holds. Repeat with the other side.

5. Allow the glue to dry completely before continuing. After the glue has dried, the cube can be collapsed flat to allow students to work at their desks.

Use the cube for organizing information on four things. Use 11" × 17" paper to make larger project cubes that you can glue other foldables onto for display. Notebook paper, photocopied sheets, magazine pictures, and current events articles can also be displayed on the larger cubes.

These cubes can be stored in plastic bag portfolios by collapsing the cubes to make them flat.

Envelope Fold

1. Fold a sheet of paper into a *taco* forming a square. Cut off the leftover piece.

2. Open the folded *taco* and refold it the opposite way forming another *taco* and an X-fold pattern.

3. Open the *taco fold* and fold the corners toward the center point of the X forming a small square.

4. Trace this square onto another sheet of paper. Cut and glue it to the inside of the envelope. Pictures can be placed under or on top of the tabs.

Use this foldable for organizing information on four things. Use it for "hidden pictures" and current events pictures. Have your classmates raise one tab at a time until they can guess what the picture represents. Number the tabs in the order in which they are to be opened.

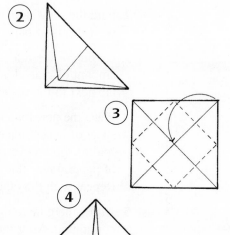

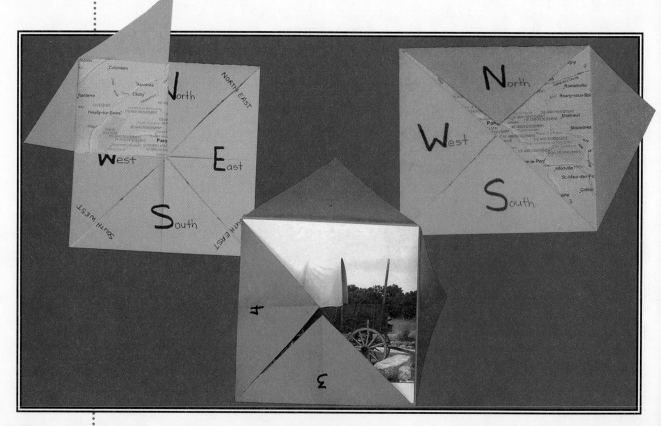

Four-Door Book

1. Make a *shutter fold* (p. 21) using a larger sheet of paper.

2. Fold the *shutter fold* in half like a *hamburger*. Crease well.

3. Open the project and cut along the two inside *valley* folds.

4. These cuts will form four doors on the inside of the project.

Use this book for organizing information on four things. When folded in half like a *hamburger*, a finished *four-door book* can be glued inside a large (11" × 17") *shutter fold* as part of a more inclusive project.

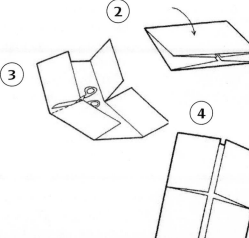

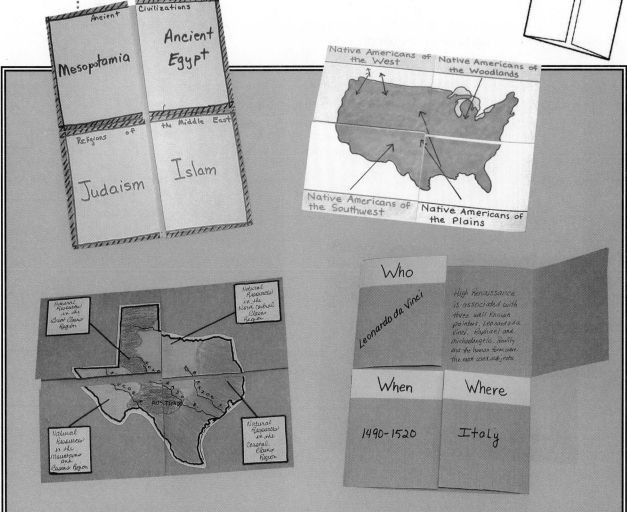

Top-Tab Book

1. Fold a sheet of paper in half like a *hamburger.* Cut the center fold, forming two half sheets.

2. Fold one of the half sheets four times. Begin by folding it in half like a *hamburger,* fold again like a *hamburger,* and finally again like a *hamburger.* This folding has formed your pattern of four rows and four columns, or 16 small squares.

3. Fold two sheets of paper in half like a *hamburger.* Cut the center folds, forming four half sheets.

4. Hold the pattern vertically and place on a half sheet of paper under the pattern. Cut the bottom right hand square out of both sheets. Set this first page aside.

5. Take a second half sheet of paper and place it under the pattern. Cut the first and second right hand squares out of both sheets. Place the second page on top of the first page.

(continued next page)

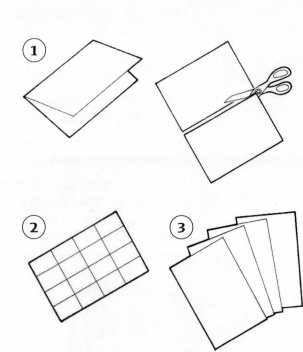

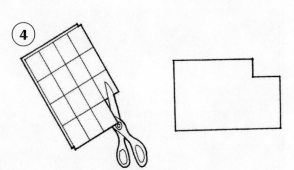

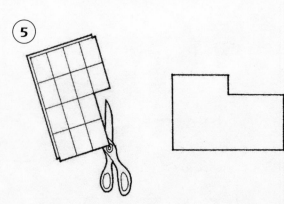

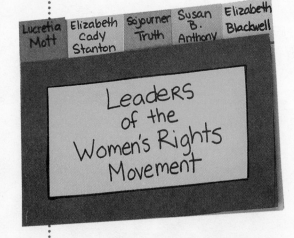

6. Take a third half sheet of paper and place it under the pattern. Cut the first, second, and third right hand squares out of both sheets. Place this third page on top of the second page.

7. Place the fourth, uncut half sheet of paper behind the three cut out sheets, leaving four aligned tabs across the top of the book. Staple several times on the left side. You can also place glue along the left paper edges and stack them together.

8. Cut a final half sheet of paper with no tabs and staple along the left side to form a cover.

Use this foldable to organize several events or characteristics of a person, place, or occurrence.

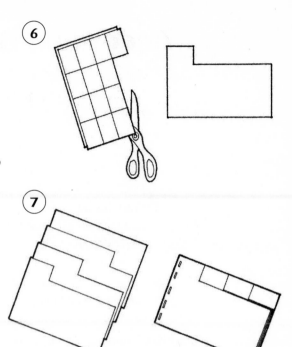

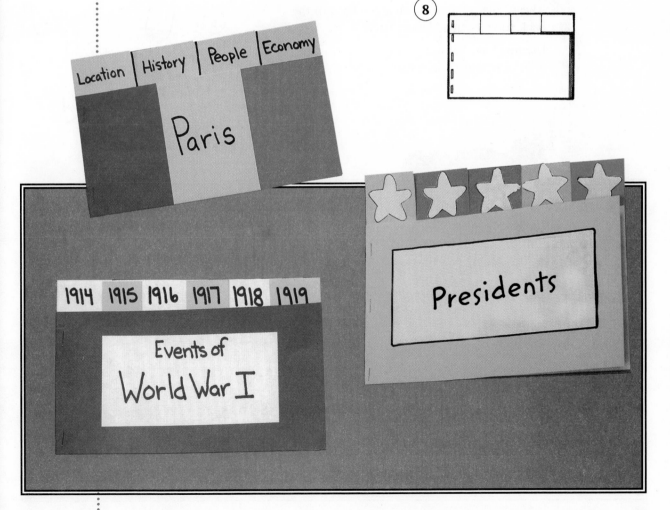

Accordion Book

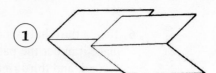

1. Fold two sheets of paper into *hamburgers*.

2. Cut the sheets of paper in half along the fold lines.

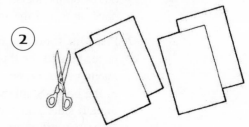

3. Fold each section of paper into *hamburgers*. However, fold one side one-half inch shorter than the other side. This will form a tab that is one-half inch long.

4. Fold this tab forward over the shorter side, and then fold it back from the shorter piece of paper. (In other words, fold it the opposite way.)

5. Glue together to form an *accordion* by gluing a straight edge of one section into the *valley* of another section.

NOTE: *Stand the sections on end to form an accordion to help students visualize how to glue them together. See illustration.*

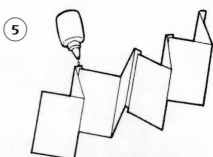

Always place the extra tab at the back of the book so you can add more pages later.

Use this book for time lines, sequencing events or information, biographies, and so on.

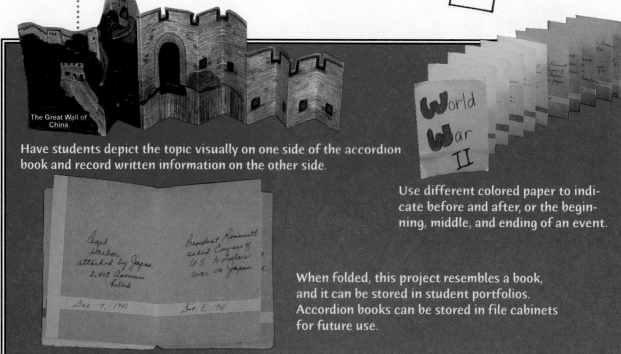

The Great Wall of China

Have students depict the topic visually on one side of the accordion book and record written information on the other side.

Use different colored paper to indicate before and after, or the beginning, middle, and ending of an event.

When folded, this project resembles a book, and it can be stored in student portfolios. Accordion books can be stored in file cabinets for future use.

Pop-Up Book

1. Fold a sheet of paper in half like a *hamburger.*

2. Beginning at the fold, or *mountain top,* cut one or more tabs.

3. Fold the tabs back and forth several times until there is a good fold line formed.

4. Partially open the *hamburger* fold and push the tabs through to the inside.

5. With one small dot of glue, glue figures for the *pop-up book* to the front of each tab. Allow the glue to dry before going on to the next step.

6. Make a cover for the book by folding another sheet of paper in half like a *hamburger.* Place glue around the outside edges of the *pop-up book* and firmly press inside the *hamburger* cover.

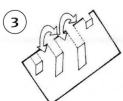

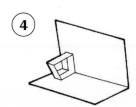

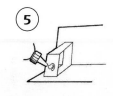

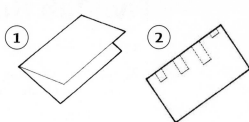

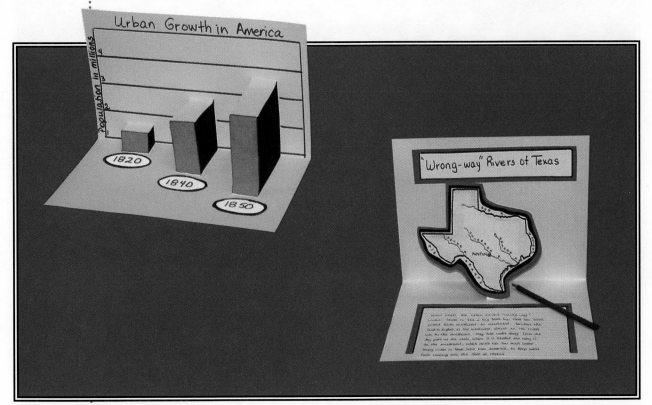

Five-Tab Book

1. Fold a sheet of paper in half like a *hot dog*.

2. Fold the paper so that one-third is exposed and two-thirds are covered.

3. Fold the two-thirds section in half.

4. Fold the one-third section (single thickness) backward to form a fold line.

The paper will be divided into fifths when opened. Use this foldable to organize information about five countries, dates, events, and so on.

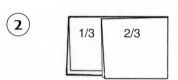
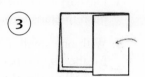

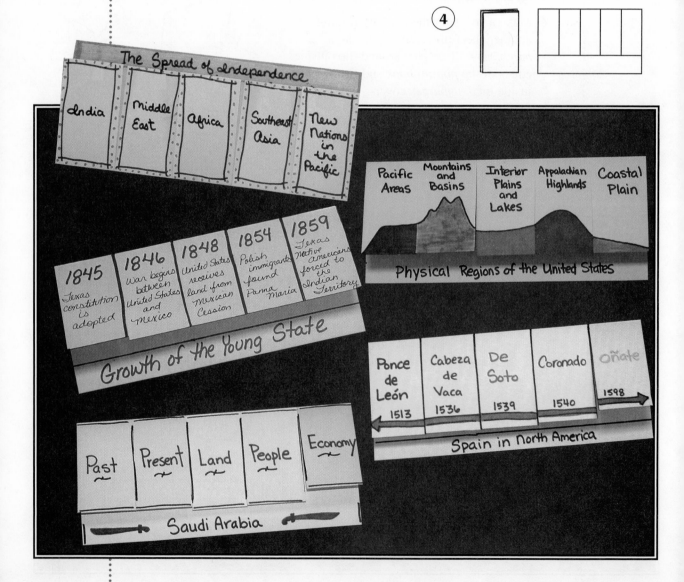

Folded Table or Chart

1. Fold a sheet of paper into the number of vertical columns needed to make the table or chart.

2. Fold the horizontal rows needed to make the table or chart.

3. Label the rows and columns.

REMEMBER: Tables are organized along vertical and horizontal axes, while charts are organized along one axis, either horizontal or vertical.

Fold the sheet of paper into as many columns or rows that you need for the particular topic.

Table

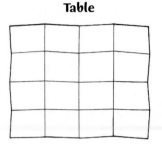

Chart

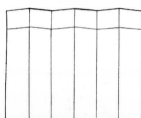

Explorer	Date	Sponsoring Country	Discovery
Marco Polo	Late 13th Century	Italy	Asia
Bartholomeu Dias	1487	Portugal	Cape of Good Hope
christopher columbus	1492	Spain	Bahamas, Cuba, Hispaniola

Chapter Two	Main Ideas	Vocabulary	Visuals or Data
Lesson 1			
Lesson 2			
Lesson 3			

Early Native americans

Hohokam	Anasazi	Mound Builders	Cahokia
Lived in present-day Arizona A.D. 300 - A.D.1200 Between Gila and Salt river valleys Used irrigation canals Pottery, carved stone, etched shells Traded with coastal people	Lived in Four Corners of Utah, Colorado, Arizona, New Mexico Built stone dwellings – Pueblos developed complex road systems between villages Built dwellings in the sides of cliffs Began leaving the area around 1300 AD. Possibly because of drought.	Lived in central North America from present day Pennsylvania to the Mississippi River valley. Built mounds similar to stone pyramids of the Maya and Aztec. Some mounds contain burial chambers. The Mounds were built by many different groups of people and objects found within indicated a widespread trade pattern.	Largest settlement of Mound builders Lived in present day Illinois. Built by the Mississippians with over 30,000 residents. The largest Mound rose nearly 100 ft and was probably the largest structure North of Mexico. Priests studied the movement of the sun and stars and there appears to have been a close link to Mexico.

New Challenges	Ronald Reagan	George Bush	Bill Clinton	George W. Bush
Party				
Foreign Policy				
Domestic Policy				

Folding a Circle Into Tenths

1. Cut a circle out of a sheet of paper. Then fold the circle in half.

2. Fold the half circle so that one-third is exposed and two-thirds are covered.

3. Fold the one-third (single thickness) backward to form a fold line.

4. Fold the two-thirds section in half.

5. The half circle will be divided into fifths. When opened, the circle will be divided into tenths.

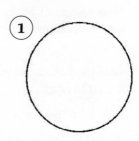

2/3

1/3

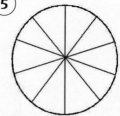

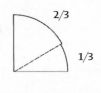

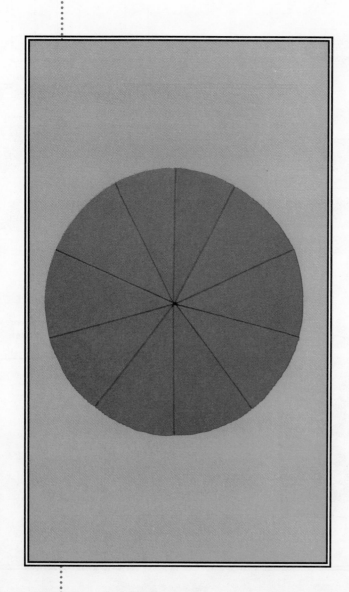

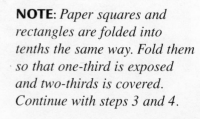

NOTE: *Paper squares and rectangles are folded into tenths the same way. Fold them so that one-third is exposed and two-thirds is covered. Continue with steps 3 and 4.*

Circle Graph

1. Cut out two circles from two sheets of paper.

2. Fold one of the circles in half on each axis, forming fourths. Cut along one of the fold lines (the radius) to the middle of each circle. Flatten the circle.

3. Place the two circles together along the cuts until they overlap completely.

4. Spin one of the circles while holding the other still. Estimate how much of each of the two (or you can add more) circles should be exposed to illustrate percentages or categories of information. Add circles to represent more than two percentages.

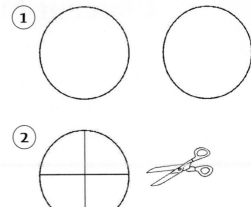

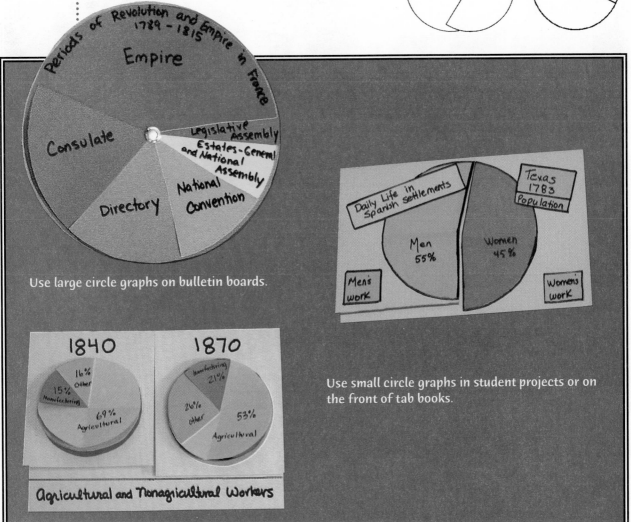

Use large circle graphs on bulletin boards.

Use small circle graphs in student projects or on the front of tab books.

Concept-Map Book

1. Fold a sheet of paper along the long or short axis, leaving a two-inch tab uncovered along the top.

2. Fold in half or in thirds.

3. Unfold and cut along the two or three inside fold lines.

Use this book to write facts about a person, place, or thing under the appropriate tab.

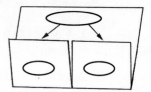

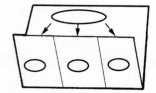

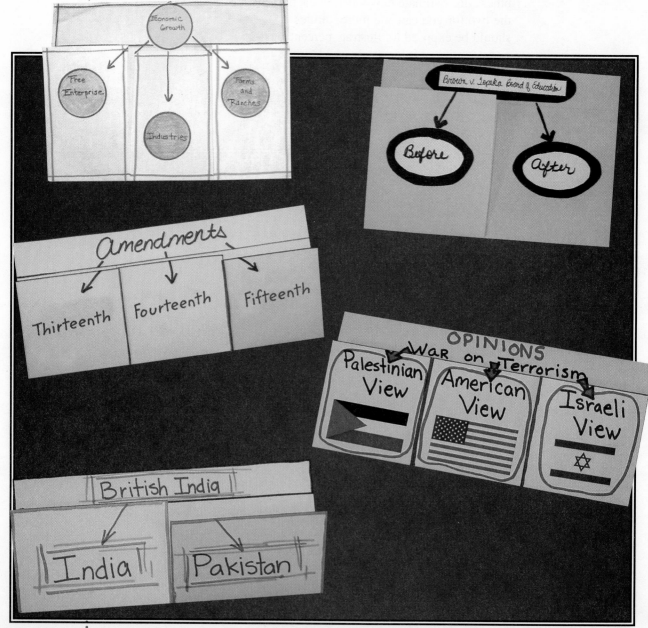

Vocabulary Book

1. Fold a sheet of notebook paper in half like a *hot dog*.

2. On one side, cut every third line. This usually results in ten tabs.

3. Label the tabs. See the illustration below for several uses.

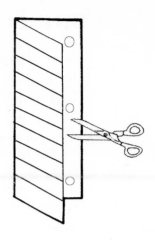

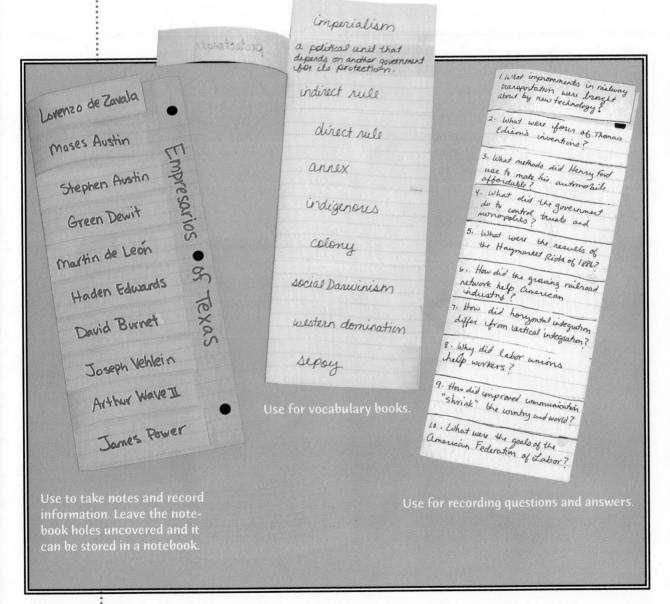

Empresarios • of Texas

Lorenzo de Zavala

Moses Austin

Stephen Austin

Green Dewit

Martin de León

Haden Edwards

David Burnet

Joseph Vehlein

Arthur Wave II

James Power

imperialism

a political unit that depends on another government for its protection.

indirect rule

direct rule

annex

indigenous

colony

social Darwinism

western domination

sepoy

Use for vocabulary books.

1. What improvements in railway transportation were brought about by new technology?

2. What were four of Thomas Edison's inventions?

3. What methods did Henry Ford use to make his automobile affordable?

4. What did the government do to control trusts and monopolies?

5. What were the results of the Haymarket Riots of 1886?

6. How did the growing railroad network help American industry?

7. How did horizontal integration differ from vertical integration?

8. Why did labor unions help workers?

9. How did improved communication "shrink" the country and world?

10. What were the goals of the American Federation of Labor?

Use to take notes and record information. Leave the notebook holes uncovered and it can be stored in a notebook.

Use for recording questions and answers.

Four-Door Diorama

1. Make a *four-door book* out of a *shutter fold* (p. 21).

2. Fold the two inside corners back to the outer edges *(mountains)* of the *shutter fold*. This will result in two *tacos* that will make the *four-door book* look like it has a shirt collar. Do the same thing to the bottom of the *four-door book*. When finished, four small triangular *tacos* have been made.

3. Form a 90-degree angle and overlap the folded triangles to make a display case that doesn't use staples or glue. (It can be collapsed for storage.)

4. Or, as illustrated, cut off all four triangles, or *tacos*. Staple or glue the sides.

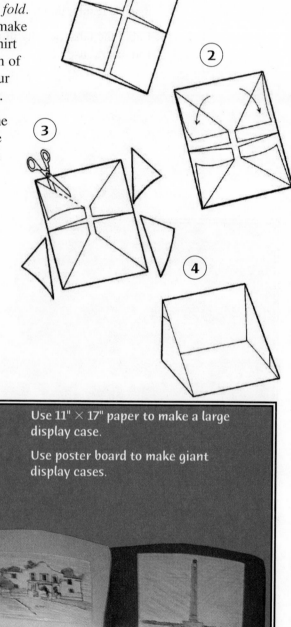

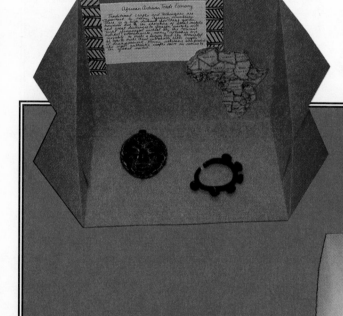

Use 11" × 17" paper to make a large display case.

Use poster board to make giant display cases.

Place display cases next to each other to compare and contrast or to sequence events or data.

Picture Frame Book

1. Fold a sheet of paper in half like a *hamburger.*

2. Open the *hamburger* and gently roll one side of the *hamburger* toward the *valley.* Try not to crease the roll.

3. Cut a rectangle out of the middle of the rolled side of the paper leaving a half-inch border, forming a frame.

4. Fold another sheet of paper in half like a *hamburger.* Apply glue to the inside border of the picture frame and place the folded, uncut sheet of paper inside.

Use this book to feature a person, place, or thing. Inside the picture frames, glue photographs, magazine pictures, computer-generated graphs, or have students sketch pictures. This book has three inside pages for writing and recording notes.

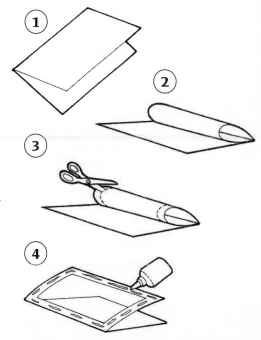

State Flower

September 11th

Speculate Why...

Life Expectancy	
Andorra	83.47
Japan	80.80
France	78.90
Israel	78.71
New Zealand	77.99
United Kingdom	77.82
United States	77.26
Chile	75.94
China	71.62
Russia	67.34
Egypt	63.69
Brazil	63.24
India	62.86
South Africa	48.09
Mozambique	36.45

Mohandas Gandhi

Display Case

1. Make a *taco* fold and cut off the leftover piece. This will result in a square.

2. Fold the square into a *shutter fold*.

3. Unfold and fold the square into another *shutter fold* perpendicular to the direction of the first. This will form a small square at each of the four corners of the sheet of paper.

4. As illustrated, cut along two fold lines on opposite sides of the large square.

5. Collapse the sides in and glue the tabs to form an open box.

How to Make a Lid

Fold another open-sided box using a square of paper one-half inch larger than the square used to make the first box. This will make a lid that fits snugly over the display box. *Example:* If the base is made out of an $8\frac{1}{2}$" paper square, make the lid out of a 9" square.

Cut a hole out of the lid and cover the opening with a cut piece of acetate used on overhead projectors. Heavy, clear plastic wrap or scraps from a laminating machine will also work. Secure the clear plastic sheet to the inside of the lid with glue or tape.

NOTE: *You can place polystyrene foam or quilt batting in the boxes to display objects. Glue the boxes onto a sheet of cardboard to make them strong enough to display heavy objects.*

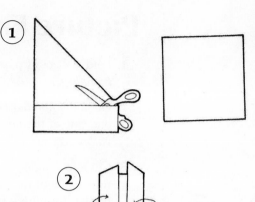

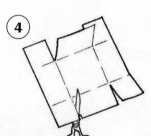

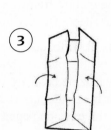

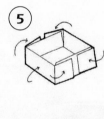

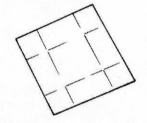

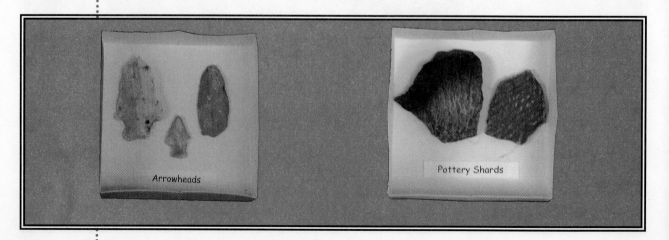

Arrowheads

Pottery Shards

Billboard Project

1. Fold all pieces of the same size of paper in half like *hamburgers*.

2. Place a line of glue at the top and bottom of one side of each folded billboard section and glue them side by side on a larger sheet of paper or poster board. If glued correctly, all doors will open from right to left.

3. Pictures, dates, words, and so on, go on the front of each billboard section. When opened, writing or drawings can be seen on the inside left of each section. The base, or the part glued to the background, is perfect for more in-depth information or definitions.

Use for time lines or for sequencing information, such as events in a war, presidents of the United States, or ratification of states.

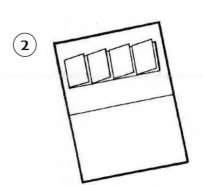

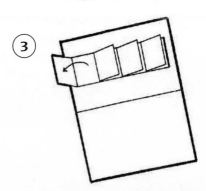

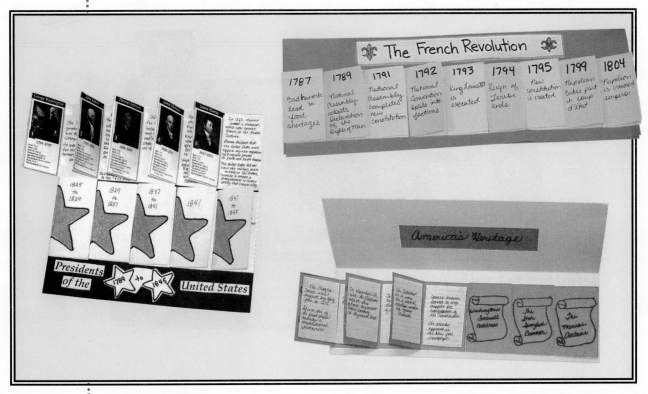

Project Board With Tabs

1. Draw a large illustration, a series of small illustrations, or write on the front of a sheet of paper.

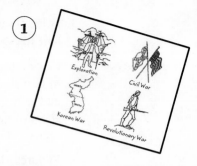

2. Pinch and slightly fold the sheet of paper at the point where a tab is desired on the illustrated sheet of paper. Cut into the paper on the fold. Cut straight in, then cut up to form an "L." When the paper is unfolded, it will form a tab with an illustration on the front.

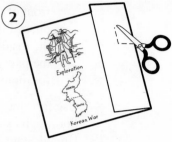

3. After all tabs have been cut, glue this front sheet onto a second sheet of paper. Place glue around all four edges and in the middle, away from tabs.

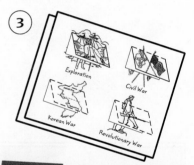

Write or draw under the tabs. If the project is made as a bulletin board using butcher paper, tape or glue smaller sheets of paper under the tabs.

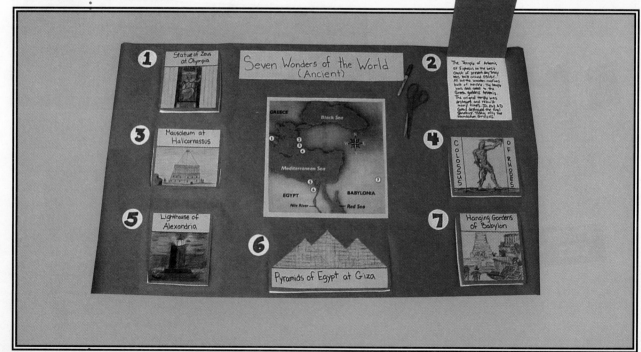

Sentence Strips

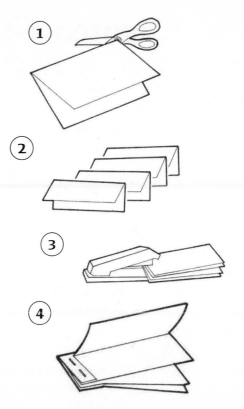

1. Take two sheets of paper and fold then into *hamburgers*. Cut along the fold lines making four half sheets. (Use as many half sheets as necessary for additional pages to your book.)

2. Fold each sheet in half like a *hot dog*.

3. Place the folds side by side and staple them together on the left side.

4. One inch from the stapled edge, cut the front page of each folded section up to the *mountain top*. These cuts form flaps that can be raised and lowered.

To make a half-cover, use a sheet of construction paper one inch longer than the book. Glue the back of the last sheet to the construction paper strip leaving one inch on the left side to fold over and cover the original staples. Staple this half-cover in place.

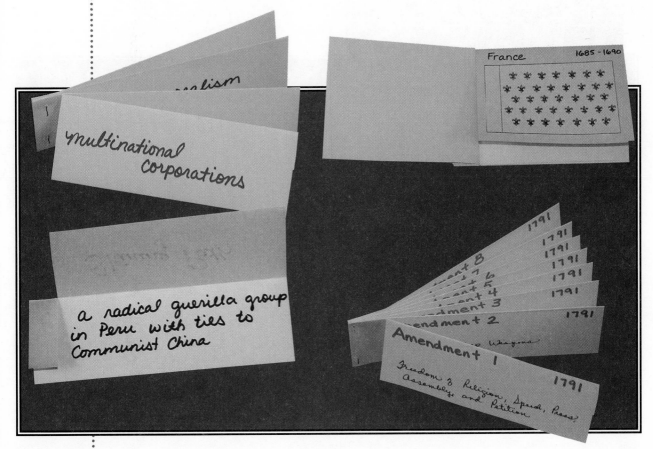

Sentence-Strip Holder

1. Fold a sheet of paper in half like a *hamburger.*

2. Open the *hamburger* and fold the two outer edges toward the *valley.* This forms a *shutter fold.*

3. Fold one of the inside edges of the shutter back to the outside fold. This fold forms a floppy L-tab.

4. Glue the floppy L-tab down to the base so that it forms a strong, straight L-tab.

5. Glue the other shutter side to the front of this L-tab. This forms a tent that is the backboard for the flashcards or student work to be displayed.

6. Fold the edge of the L-tab up one-quarter to one-half inch to form a lip that will keep the student work from slipping off the holder.

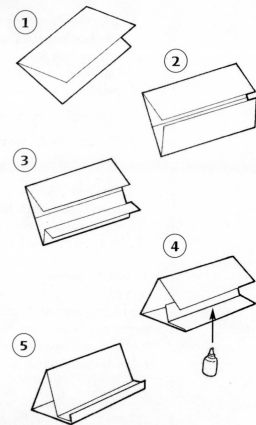

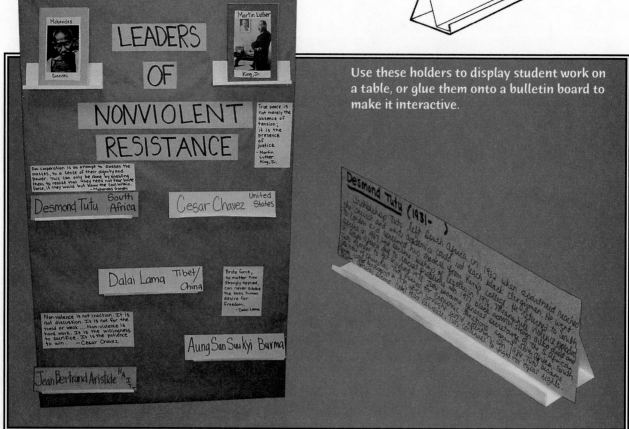

Use these holders to display student work on a table, or glue them onto a bulletin board to make it interactive.

Forward-Backward Book

1. Stack three or more sheets of paper. On the top sheet, trace a large circle.

2. With the papers still stacked, cut out the circles.

3. Staple the paper circles together along the left-hand side to create a circular booklet.

4. Label the cover and takes notes on the pages that open to the right.

5. Turn the book upside down and label the back. Takes notes on the pages that open to the right.

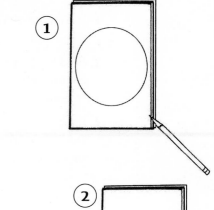

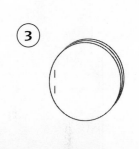

Front

Back

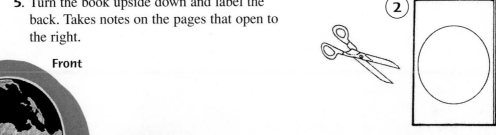

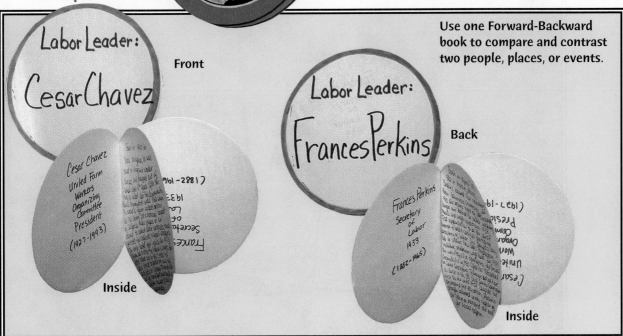

Front

Back

Inside

Inside

Use one Forward-Backward book to compare and contrast two people, places, or events.

Three-Pocket Book

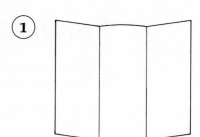

1. Fold a horizontal sheet of paper (11" × 17") into thirds.

2. Fold the bottom edge up two inches and crease well. Glue the outer edges of the two-inch tab to create three pockets.

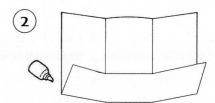

3. Label each pocket. Use these pockets to hold notes taken on index cards or quarter sheets of paper.

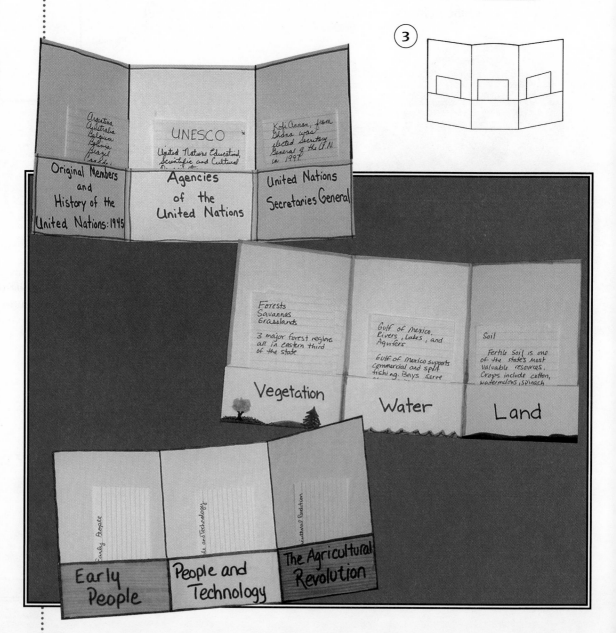

FOLDABLES™

Chapter Activities for

Civics Today
Citizenship, Economics, & You

The pages that follow contain chapter-specific Foldables activities to use with *Civics Today: Citizenship, Economics, and You*. Included are a Chapter Summary, a reproduction of the Foldables Study Organizer that appears on each chapter opener in the textbook, and a Follow-Up Foldables Activity. Use the Follow-Up Activity after students have studied each chapter. Students are asked to use the Foldables they have created and completed during the study of each chapter to review important chapter concepts and prepare for the chapter test.

Alternative Foldables activities are also included for every chapter. Use these activities during the study of each chapter or as chapter review activities. The Student Study Tip provides reading, writing, and test-taking strategies that you can share with your students throughout the course.

Chapter-Specific

FOLDABLES

Citizenship and Government in a Democracy

CHAPTER SUMMARY

Democratic governments perform necessary functions so citizens can live together peacefully. Our government protects our rights and provides us with benefits. Without our government there would be no police officers, libraries, parks, schools, court system, or water system. American democracy is most effective if its residents are active citizens. The U.S. Constitution established the rights of citizenship and the pathway for those born outside the United States to become citizens—a process called naturalization. The United States has a long tradition of immigration and has developed into a society that benefits greatly from its diversity.

CHAPTER PREVIEW

Organizing Information Study Foldable *Make the following foldable to help you organize what you learn about citizenship and government in a democracy.*

Step 1 *Collect 2 sheets of paper and place them about 1 inch apart.*

Keep the edges straight.

Step 2 *Fold up the bottom edges of the paper to form 4 tabs.*

This makes all tabs the same size.

Step 3 *When all the tabs are the same size, crease the paper to hold the tabs in place and staple the sheets together. Label each tab as shown.*

Staple together along the fold.

Reading and Writing *As you read the chapter, write the main ideas presented in each of the three sections of the chapter under the tabs of your foldable.*

CHAPTER REVIEW

Foldables Follow-Up Activity

Have students use the information on their foldables as a foundation for a small research project about immigrants in their community. Direct them to newspaper and Internet resources that discuss the immigrants, the jobs they have, their efforts at naturalization, and their contributions to the community. Ask students to find articles about festivals or other events that introduce others to the customs of immigrants. For example, many cities have Italian Festivals or Greek Festivals. Have students compile their findings in a two-page report.

Alternative Activities for Chapter 1

EXPLAINING

Have students explore the How and Why of citizenship in this foldable. Students should identify the two main ways one can become a citizen and then explain each under the appropriate tabs of their foldables. They should use the third section of their foldables to explain why citizenship is important. Lead a class discussion about the importance of committed citizens to a democratic nation.

Citizenship: How and Why
Birth
Naturalization
Importance

Key Terms
Democracy
Immigrant
Patriotism

DEFINING

Remind students that they are individuals and that each of them interacts with their community in different ways. Have students choose three Key Terms from the chapter, write them on their foldables, and define them under the appropriate tabs. Then have them write two to three sentences that describe what each term means to them in their lives. Ask for volunteers to read their sentences.

Student Study Tip

Point out that political cartoonists use pictures to present their opinions about issues. They often use symbols like Uncle Sam to represent something else. Have students analyze the cartoons in this chapter and throughout the textbook. They should ask themselves: What symbols are used? What ideas are the cartoonists presenting? This will help students think critically and see others' viewpoints.

Chapter 1

FOLDABLES

Roots of American Democracy

CHAPTER SUMMARY

The first colonists in America cherished the traditions of representative government that they had known in England. When Great Britain began exerting tighter control over the American colonies, the colonists resisted in years of protests that resulted in the Revolutionary War. The Declaration of Independence and Articles of Confederation established the United States as a sovereign, or independent, country. Despite its weaknesses, the Confederation Congress was able to win the Revolutionary War. Independence did not put an end to America's struggles, however, and in 1787, delegates were sent to revise the Articles.

CHAPTER PREVIEW

FOLDABLES™
Study Organizer

Sequencing Events Study Foldable *Make this foldable to help you sequence the events that led to the creation of our American democratic system.*

Step 1 *Fold two sheets of paper in half from top to bottom.*

Step 2 *Turn the papers and cut each in half.*

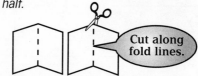

Cut along fold lines.

Step 3 *Fold the four pieces in half from top to bottom.*

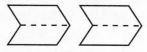

Step 4 *Tape the ends of the pieces together (overlapping the edges very slightly) to make an accordion time line.*

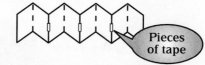

Pieces of tape

Reading and Writing *As you read the chapter, sequence the events that led to the writing of the Declaration of Independence and the formation of America's first government by writing a date and event on each part of the time line.*

CHAPTER REVIEW

Foldables Follow-Up Activity

Ask students to use their foldables to write a narrative of American independence. Instruct them to use the events they have written on their foldables to write the narrative as if they were colonists involved in early colonial government. Remind students of the importance of smooth transitions and identifying causes and effects in telling their story.

Alternative Activities for Chapter 2

SEQUENCING

Have students create foldables that identify examples of self-government that led to the Articles of Confederation. The examples may include documents such as the Mayflower Compact or important meetings such as the First Continental Congress. On each segment of this foldable, students should identify the event or document and explain why it was important to the development of representative government.

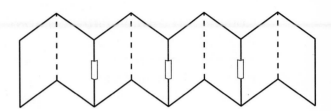

ANALYZING

Have students list the weaknesses of the Articles of Confederation on their foldables. Students should then place a star next to the one they think is the weakest and write a short explanation of why. Once students have completed their foldables, lead a class discussion about the weaknesses and the problems they caused for the new nation.

Student Study Tip

To improve reading retention, have students quiz themselves on material immediately after they read it. Each time students reach a new subject head, they should ask themselves what they learned in the previous subsection. This will ensure that they link the whole section and chapter together and read more carefully.

Chapter 2 **FOLDABLES**

The Constitution

CHAPTER SUMMARY

The United States Constitution established our nation's government. Two opposing plans—the Virginia Plan and the New Jersey Plan—were presented at the Constitutional Convention. The Great Compromise settled the structure of Congress but not the issue of representation in Congress. The Three-Fifths Compromise solved this by counting every five enslaved persons as three free persons. The writers of the Constitution set up a process to add amendments. This ensured that the document would be adaptable as the nation went through changes. The Constitution embodied several key principles, including popular sovereignty, rule of law, separation of powers, and checks and balances.

CHAPTER PREVIEW

FOLDABLES™
Study Organizer

Summarizing Information Study Foldable *Make and use this study guide to record the main ideas of the chapter and information on the United States Constitution.*

Step 1 *Fold a sheet of paper in half from top to bottom.*

Step 2 *Fold the paper in half again from side to side.*

Reading and Writing *As you read the chapter, record events that led to the formation, ratification, and implementation of the United States Constitution.*

Step 3 *Label your foldable as shown.*

CHAPTER REVIEW

Foldables Follow-Up Activity

After students have created their foldables, have them write a quiz for a classmate. Using their journal foldables, students should write two to three paragraphs about the Constitutional Convention, leaving blanks for their classmate to fill in. They should also write an answer key. Students could leave blanks for Key Terms or significant names associated with the convention and the Constitution. After students have traded quizzes and graded them, they should discuss what they learned and ask any questions they may have.

Alternative Activities for Chapter 3

DESCRIBING

Have students use the library or the Internet to find information on the different delegates to the Constitutional Convention. Have students choose a delegate and write a short biography of him in their foldable. Biographies should contain basic facts about the delegate and what he contributed to the convention. Display the biographies around the classroom or combine them into a book titled "Founders of the Nation."

EVALUATING

Have students create a foldable that discusses one of the underlying principles of the Constitution. Instruct them to select one of the principles in Section 4 and list possible points of debate that might have taken place among the delegates. Suggest that students use one side of the foldable for "pro" arguments and the facing side for "con" arguments for their particular principle. Lead a class discussion on the good and bad aspects of each principle.

Student Study Tip

As students are learning about the Constitution of the United States, suggest they take time to read the full text on pages 60–81 in their textbooks. Encourage them to read the "What It Means" boxes in the margins for better clarity on the meaning of each article and section. Remind students that the Constitution has been the fundamental law of the United States for more than 200 years.

Chapter 3 FOLDABLES

The Bill of Rights

CHAPTER SUMMARY

The Bill of Rights—the first 10 amendments to the U.S. Constitution—guarantees certain basic rights to all Americans. The First Amendment protects five basic freedoms: freedom of religion, freedom of speech, freedom of the press, freedom of assembly, and freedom to petition the government. There are limits to First Amendment freedoms, because otherwise one person could infringe on another's freedoms. The other nine amendments guarantee the right to fair legal treatment, as well as other rights and liberties. The amendments adopted after the Bill of Rights extended liberties and voting rights to African Americans, women, and other minority groups. However, some groups still did not have equal rights. African Americans, therefore, organized a civil rights movement to gain equality.

CHAPTER PREVIEW

Evaluating Information Study Foldable *Make this foldable to write questions and answers as you study the Bill of Rights.*

Step 1 *Write a summary of the Bill of Rights on one side of a sheet of paper.*

Step 2 *Fold the sheet of paper into thirds from top to bottom.*

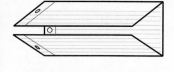

Step 3 *Unfold, turn the paper over (to the clean side), and label as shown.*

Reading and Writing *As you read about the Bill of Rights, write down three main questions under each heading. Then write an answer to each question.*

CHAPTER REVIEW

Foldables Follow-Up Activity

Organize students into small groups. Have them take turns asking the other group members the questions they have written on their foldables. The student asking the questions should not share his or her answers until each student has tried to give the answer. After each student has asked his or her questions, have students work together in their small groups to create a collage with magazine pictures or sketches about what the Bill of Rights means to them.

Alternative Activities for Chapter 4

ORGANIZING

Instruct students to choose three of the first 10 amendments to the U.S. Constitution and write them on their foldables. Ask them to write a couple of descriptive words under each amendment so they can more easily remember each amendment. For example, they could write *double jeopardy* and *silent* for the Fifth Amendment. Then ask volunteers to share their words until all 10 amendments are covered.

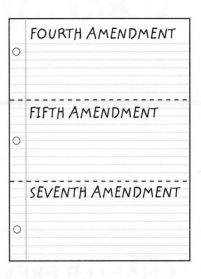

FOURTH AMENDMENT

FIFTH AMENDMENT

SEVENTH AMENDMENT

Civil Rights
Act of 1957

Voting Rights
Act of 1965

Open Housing
Act of 1968

DESCRIBING

Have students write three landmark acts of the civil rights movement on their foldables. They can refer to the chart on page 114 in their textbook for this information. Ask students to do research on the Internet to find additional information about the three acts they have chosen. Point out to students how recent some of the acts are, and initiate a discussion on civil rights issues that still exist today.

Student Study Tip

Share the following tips with your students about taking notes from their textbooks. First, they should read one section without taking notes to focus on understanding the material. Second, they should locate the main ideas and restate them in their own words. Finally, they should write the paraphrased ideas in their notebooks and review them daily.

Chapter 4 FOLDABLES

The Citizen and the Community

CHAPTER SUMMARY

It is the combination of rights, responsibilities, and duties that characterize what it means to be a citizen of a free, democratic society. Along with the privileges of being a U.S. citizen come certain duties and responsibilities. Some are legal, such as paying taxes and obeying laws, while others are voluntary, such as participating in the political process by voting. There is also the need for citizen involvement because the government has limited resources. Volunteerism—the practice of offering time and services to others without payment—helps make communities better places to live.

CHAPTER PREVIEW

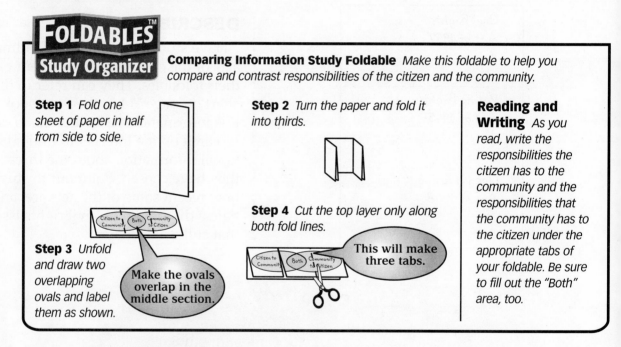

FOLDABLES™ Study Organizer

Comparing Information Study Foldable *Make this foldable to help you compare and contrast responsibilities of the citizen and the community.*

Step 1 *Fold one sheet of paper in half from side to side.*

Step 2 *Turn the paper and fold it into thirds.*

Step 3 *Unfold and draw two overlapping ovals and label them as shown.*

Make the ovals overlap in the middle section.

Citizen to Community   Both   Community to Citizen

Step 4 *Cut the top layer only along both fold lines.*

This will make three tabs.

Citizen to Community   Both   Community to Citizen

Reading and Writing *As you read, write the responsibilities the citizen has to the community and the responsibilities that the community has to the citizen under the appropriate tabs of your foldable. Be sure to fill out the "Both" area, too.*

CHAPTER REVIEW

Foldables Follow-Up Activity

Organize students into pairs. Instruct each pair to think of specific responsibilities they have to their communities. They should then agree on the most important one, such as respecting others' rights, and create a mini poster with pictures of examples of how they could carry out the responsibility. For example, they could include a picture of someone throwing trash in a trash can instead of littering.

Alternative Activities for Chapter 5

COMPARING

Have students write *Duties, Respon-sibilities,* and *Both* on the Venn diagrams on their foldables. Students should read through Section 1 of this chapter to find ways in which citizens' duties and responsibilities differ and ways in which they are similar. After students have completed their foldables, ask for volunteers to give examples of each.

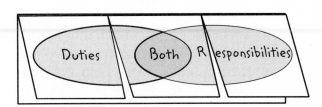

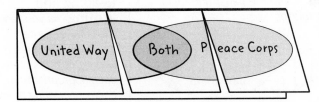

EXPLAINING

Explain to students that although vol-unteer organizations have the same ulti-mate goal of helping the community, whether it is a local or a national organ-ization, there are differences in what each does. Have students choose two volunteer organizations from their text-book and compare them on their fold-ables. Ask several students to share information about the groups they chose. Make sure students understand the purposes and goals of several organizations.

Student Study Tip

As students are learning new material, remind them to use the images in each chapter to help them better understand the material. Have stu-dents examine the photographs and graphics in this chapter and explain why they think each is included. Once students understand that graph-ics have a specific purpose, the graphics will offer more instructional value. Encourage stu-dents to summarize the information presented in the graphics as they take notes.

Chapter 5

FOLDABLES

Congress

CHAPTER SUMMARY

Congress is made up of 435 representatives and 100 senators. Members of each political party select their own leaders and work mainly in committees to carry out their duties. In addition to passing laws, Congress has other powers such as oversight, investigation, and approval of the president's nominees. In matters of legislation, Congress follows strict procedures to guide a bill into becoming a law. If committees in the House and the Senate approve a bill, it goes to the full House or Senate. If the bill passes in both houses, the Congress sends it to the president for approval.

CHAPTER PREVIEW

FOLDABLES™
Study Organizer

Summarizing Information Study Foldable *Make the following foldable to help you organize and summarize what you learn about the U.S. Congress.*

Step 1 *Fold a sheet of paper in half from side to side.*

Step 2 *Turn the paper and fold it into fourths.*

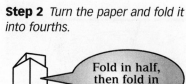
Fold in half, then fold in half again.

Reading and Writing *As you read the chapter, write down what you learn about Congress under each appropriate tab. Focus on writing main ideas and supporting details you find in the chapter.*

Step 3 *Unfold and cut up along the three fold lines, cutting through just the top layer.*

Make four tabs.

Step 4 *Label your foldable as shown.*

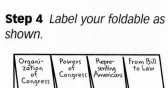
Organization of Congress | Powers of Congress | Representing Americans | From Bill to Law

CHAPTER REVIEW

Foldables Follow-Up Activity

Organize the class into groups of four, and have each group use their foldables to create a poster with the information they know about Congress. Posters should show diagrams, tables, and flowcharts to illustrate the structure and work of Congress. Suggest that students use arrows to show the connections between different congressional bodies and the powers they have. Display the posters around the classroom.

Alternative Activities for Chapter 6

IDENTIFYING

Have students explore the inner workings of Congress by creating this foldable. Students should identify four types of congressional leaders. They should then write what they learn under each appropriate tab, including details about each leader's responsibilities. Ask students to research to find out who currently holds each leadership position.

Speaker of the House	president pro tempore	floor leaders	"whips"

SUMMARIZING

Instruct students to summarize the four steps of how a bill becomes a law. Students should list each step and summarize what happens during each stage of the process under the appropriate tab of their foldables. Discuss with the class why the process is so complicated, and how the process ensures that no bills are passed without serious consideration and debate.

Committee Action	Floor Action	Conference Action	Passage

Student Study Tip

There are several review tools that students can use in order to prepare for tests. Students can create study checklists to organize the material into manageable chunks. They can outline the chapter and then quiz themselves on the main ideas of the outline. Students can also create flash cards for Key Terms and other concepts or events.

Chapter 6 FOLDABLES

The President and the Executive Branch

CHAPTER SUMMARY

Every four years, Americans cast their votes for a president and vice president. The U.S. Constitution set up an indirect method of election, called the Electoral College. The first four executive departments were the attorney general and the secretaries of state, war, and treasury, but the executive branch has since grown to 15 departments. This branch of government is responsible for carrying out the many programs that Congress has created to serve the American people. The Executive Office of the President (EOP) is the president's administration. The EOP helps the president manage the many complex tasks of the executive branch and its thousands of employees.

CHAPTER PREVIEW

Know-Want-Learn Study Foldable *Make this foldable to determine what you already know, what you want to know, and what you learn about the executive branch of government.*

Step 1 *Fold a sheet of paper into thirds from top to bottom.*

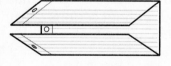

Step 2 *Turn the paper horizontally, unfold, and label the three columns as shown.*

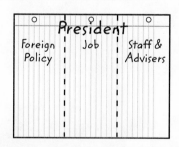

Reading and Writing *Before you read, write down what you already know and what you want to know under each heading. As you read the chapter, record what you learn.*

CHAPTER REVIEW

Foldables Follow-Up Activity

Direct students to Internet resources such as www.whitehouse.gov to find information about President George W. Bush and his administration. Students should use the three categories on their foldables as an outline, and write an essay that describes the current administration. Encourage students to cite things unique to the Bush Administration such as the war on terrorism and individuals on his personal staff.

Alternative Activities for Chapter 7

ANALYZING

Have students create a foldable that summarizes the roles that President George W. Bush has during the war on terrorism. Students should choose three roles of the president and write these on their foldables. Under each heading, students should explain the role of the president and provide specific examples of what the president is currently doing in that role. Lead a class discussion about the importance of the president, both practically and symbolically.

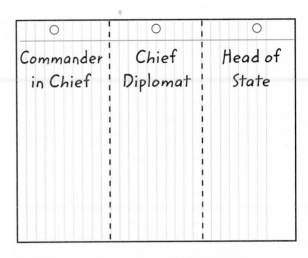

Commander in Chief	Chief Diplomat	Head of State

Executive Agencies	Government Corporations	Regulatory Commissions

DRAWING CONCLUSIONS

The executive branch contains many agencies outside of the executive departments and the EOP. Students should write the three types of independent agencies on their foldables and provide examples of each. In small groups, ask students to discuss how they think the example agencies affect their daily lives. Have groups share their conclusions with the rest of the class.

Student Study Tip

As students read the chapters in their textbook, have them create an information bank at the beginning of each section in their notes. Students should ask themselves what they think they will learn in each section. Then suggest they go back to their information banks after class lectures and discussion to fill in what they learned.

Chapter 7 **FOLDABLES**

The Judicial Branch

CHAPTER SUMMARY

The American judicial system is one of the nation's most important institutions. The courts that make up the judicial branch see that our nation's laws are justly enforced. Three levels of federal courts—district courts, appeals courts, and the Supreme Court—handle a wide array of cases every year and try to ensure that everyone in the United States receives equal justice under the law. The Supreme Court's decisions have wide-ranging effects because court justices interpret the meaning of the U.S. Constitution. Each year the Supreme Court gets more than 7,000 applications, and selects fewer than 200 cases to hear. All accepted cases go through a series of steps: written arguments, oral arguments, conference, opinion writing, and announcement.

CHAPTER PREVIEW

Compare and Contrast Study Foldable *Make this foldable to help you determine similarities and differences between the federal courts and the Supreme Court of the United States.*

Step 1 *Fold one sheet of paper in half from top to bottom.*

Step 2 *Fold it in half again, from side to side.*

Reading and Writing *As you read, write information under each appropriate tab to help you compare and contrast the purpose and organization of these courts.*

Step 3 *Unfold the paper once, label it, and cut up the fold of the top flap only.*

This cut will make two tabs.

CHAPTER REVIEW

Foldables Follow-Up Activity

Organize students into small groups to research three Supreme Court cases. They should use computer databases at the library or look on the Internet for information about these cases. Have them select one recent case and find specific newspaper articles about it. Have groups share their cases with the class. Ask the class why they think the Supreme Court accepted each case. Then ask students if they agree or disagree with the Court's decision to hear each case and why.

Alternative Activities for Chapter 8

COMPARING

Have students create and complete this foldable by writing information about how *judges* are selected under one tab, and information about how *justices* are selected under the other tab. They should then place stars with colored pencils or markers next to the items that are the same and an "X" next to those things that are different between the two selection processes.

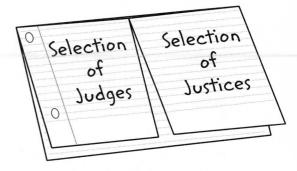

SUMMARIZING

Tell students that although the Supreme Court has a great deal of power, there are limits to this power. Have students list the powers of the Court on one half of their foldables, and then list the limits to these powers on the other half. They should study Section 3 of this chapter to find this information. Then hold a class discussion and write students' responses on the board. Encourage students to add any important information to their foldables that they may not have included.

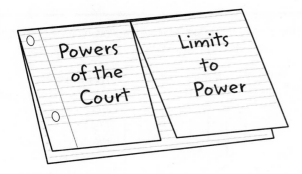

Student Study Tip

Encourage students to spend some time becoming familiar with using library resources. Students should explore these various types of reference books: encyclopedias, biographical dictionaries, atlases, and almanacs. Students may use card catalogs, periodical guides, and/or computer databases to help them find the information they need.

Chapter 8 FOLDABLES

Political Parties and Politics

CHAPTER SUMMARY

Shortly after our nation was formed, political leaders formed parties in an attempt to gain control of decision making in the government. During most of American history, there have been two major political parties. For this reason, the United States is said to have a two-party system. Today's major parties are the Democrats and the Republicans. Each party has a national committee and congressional campaign committees. Political parties nominate candidates through a nomination process of direct primaries. Political parties campaign for their candidates by raising money, informing voters, and getting people to vote.

CHAPTER PREVIEW

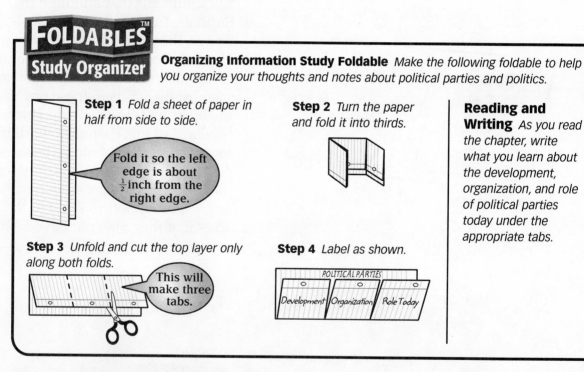

FOLDABLES™ Study Organizer

Organizing Information Study Foldable *Make the following foldable to help you organize your thoughts and notes about political parties and politics.*

Step 1 *Fold a sheet of paper in half from side to side.*

Fold it so the left edge is about ½ inch from the right edge.

Step 2 *Turn the paper and fold it into thirds.*

Step 3 *Unfold and cut the top layer only along both folds.*

This will make three tabs.

Step 4 *Label as shown.*

POLITICAL PARTIES
Development | Organization | Role Today

Reading and Writing *As you read the chapter, write what you learn about the development, organization, and role of political parties today under the appropriate tabs.*

CHAPTER REVIEW

Foldables Follow-Up Activity

After students have completed their foldables, ask them to write an outline on the development, organization, and role of political parties today. Make sure they are familiar with the format of outlines before they begin. Encourage them to do this often throughout the study of a chapter as a way to reinforce new material they learn.

Alternative Activities for Chapter 9

CATEGORIZING

Have students write what they know and what they learn from the chapter about the Democratic Party, the Republican Party, and third parties under the appropriate tabs of their foldables. Then have them research to find at least five individuals who are affiliated with each party. Have them write a one-page biographical essay on one of these individuals and be sure to include that person's contributions to his or her party.

EXPLAINING

Students should define each of the following on their foldables: *direct primary, closed primary,* and *open primary.* Then have them add additional facts for each under the appropriate tab. Ask students to write two fill-in-the-blank sentences for each term and then trade with a partner to complete the other's sentences. They should return the sentences to the original writer for grading.

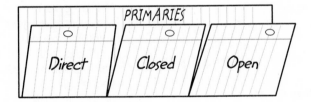

Student Study Tip

Remind students that it is important to think before writing an essay. They should ask themselves: What is the topic of the essay? What type of essay should I be writing? Is it argumentative, biographical, or other? What are the length requirements? What should I be sure to include in my essay? If students are not under a time constraint, encourage them to write several drafts before writing the final essay.

Chapter 9 FOLDABLES

Voting and Elections

CHAPTER SUMMARY

Voting is an important right and responsibility of citizenship. After registering to vote, citizens go to a polling place to cast their ballots. The best way to prepare to vote is to stay informed about candidates and public issues. Elections are held year-round, but presidential and congressional elections are held in November. Political campaigns require millions of dollars. The purpose of campaigns is to convince the public to vote for a particular candidate. While there are rules for how a candidate funds a campaign, many agree that campaign finance reform is needed.

CHAPTER PREVIEW

FOLDABLES™
Study Organizer

Analyzing Information Study Foldable *Make this foldable to help you answer questions about voting and elections.*

Step 1 *Mark the midpoint of a side edge of one sheet of paper. Then fold the outside edges in to touch the midpoint.*

Step 2 *Fold in half from side to side.*

Step 3 *Open and cut along the inside fold lines to form four tabs.*

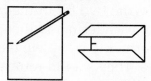

Cut along the fold lines on both sides.

Step 4 *Label as shown.*

Who can vote? | What are election campaigns?
When are elections held? | How are campaigns paid for?

Reading and Writing *As you read the chapter, ask yourself the questions labeled on the foldable. As you read each section, find the answer to each question. Record your answers under the appropriate tab.*

CHAPTER REVIEW

Foldables Follow-Up Activity

Students have learned the importance of voting and many have probably heard or seen a public service announcement. Have students write public service announcements for each foldable category. The four short scripts should answer the questions on the foldable, provide details about the electoral process, and end with a reminder for citizens to vote.

Alternative Activities for Chapter 10

SEQUENCING

An election involves several steps. Have students complete this foldable by providing details of how each step is carried out under the appropriate tab. Then have students research locations in their community where a voter can register to vote, cast a vote, and acquire an absentee ballot. Students should also find out where the vote is counted. Then ask students to find a newspaper article that gives the results of a recent election.

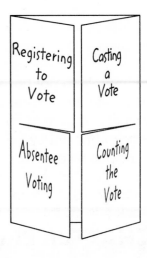

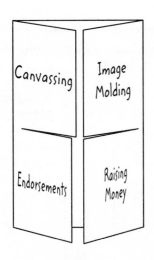

DESCRIBING

In this foldable, students should describe four ways that campaign workers assist candidates who run for office. Organize students into small groups to create a poster for a candidate as if they are campaign workers. (Students could choose a fictional candidate or someone already in office.) Remind them to highlight the candidate's best qualities on the poster and to think of a catchy slogan.

Student Study Tip

While taking tests, advise your students to answer the questions they know first and then go back to the harder questions. They will gain some confidence this way and be able to focus on the more difficult questions. They will also avoid finishing a test with unanswered questions for which they knew the answers.

Chapter 10 FOLDABLES

Influencing Government

CHAPTER SUMMARY

Public opinion includes the ideas and attitudes that most people hold about elected officials, candidates, government, and political issues. Politicians and government officials know that public support is necessary to stay in office and achieve their goals. The mass media also play a vital role in politics and government in the United States, linking the people to their elected officials. Interest groups are another important part of our democratic process because their primary goal is to influence public policy, which is the course of action the government takes in response to an issue or problem. Citizens join together in various kinds of interest groups to pool their skills, knowledge, and resources to influence decisions made by politicians and government officials.

CHAPTER PREVIEW

Summarizing Information Study Foldable *Make this foldable to help you take notes on groups, organizations, and institutions that influence our government.*

Step 1 *Fold a sheet of paper into thirds from top to bottom.*

Step 2 *Turn the paper horizontally, unfold, and label the three columns as shown.*

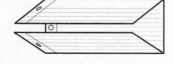

Reading and Writing *Take notes as you read the chapter. Place your notes under the heads of the appropriate columns.*

CHAPTER REVIEW

Foldables Follow-Up Activity

Organize students into small groups. Have students participate in a read-aloud of their foldables. Tell them to discuss each of the three major ways of influencing government that they have listed on their foldables. After the discussion, ask students which they think has the *most* influence on government and why. Tally the votes on the board, and then discuss students' choices. For extra credit, ask students to write a short article as a journalist reporting on a public problem, such as pollution or a corrupt government leader.

Alternative Activities for Chapter 11

IDENTIFYING

Have students write the three components of public opinion—*Direction, Intensity,* and *Stability*—on their foldables. Ask students to explain and give examples of each component and write this information under the appropriate heading. Encourage them to think of their own examples in addition to the ones given in the textbook. Ask for volunteers to share their examples with the rest of the class.

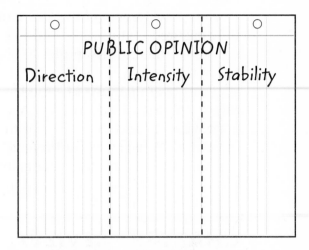

PUBLIC OPINION		
Direction	Intensity	Stability

MASS MEDIA		
Television	Internet	Newspaper

DETERMINING CAUSE AND EFFECT

Have students choose three types of mass media and write these on their foldables. Then have them think of a way each type has affected the way they think and view things. On a separate sheet of paper, have students write two to three paragraphs about the important role of the mass media. Ask: Why is the mass media such a powerful influence on public opinion? Make sure they cite specific reasons.

Student Study Tip

Point out to students that it is important when reading about political events or other events to think about cause and effect. Students should be able to recognize what happened and know why it happened. Note that most effects have more than one cause and that causes can have more than one effect. Show students several examples of cause-and-effect charts.

Chapter 11 FOLDABLES

State Government

CHAPTER SUMMARY

When the Framers of the U.S. Constitution created a federal system, they ensured that power would be shared between the national and state governments. Examples of shared, or concurrent, powers include the power to levy taxes, borrow money, and establish courts. State legislatures operate much like the U.S. Congress, but they also have the important task of apportioning election districts. Both houses must approve a bill and the governor must sign it before it becomes a law. A governor's most important role is that of the state's chief executive. In this role, the governor is responsible for carrying out the laws of the state. State courts are organized in a three-tier system similar in structure to the federal judiciary.

CHAPTER PREVIEW

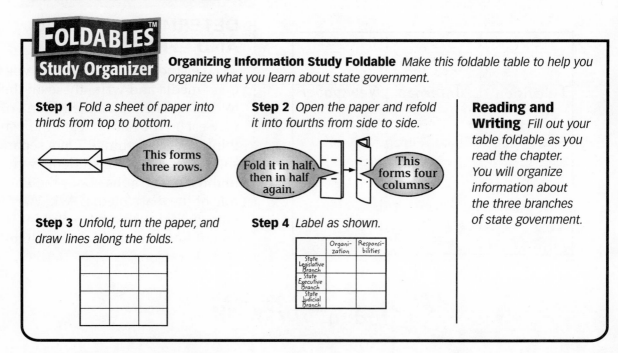

FOLDABLES™
Study Organizer

Organizing Information Study Foldable *Make this foldable table to help you organize what you learn about state government.*

Step 1 *Fold a sheet of paper into thirds from top to bottom.*

This forms three rows.

Step 2 *Open the paper and refold it into fourths from side to side.*

Fold it in half, then in half again.

This forms four columns.

Reading and Writing *Fill out your table foldable as you read the chapter. You will organize information about the three branches of state government.*

Step 3 *Unfold, turn the paper, and draw lines along the folds.*

Step 4 *Label as shown.*

	Organi-zation	Responsi-bilities
State Legislative Branch		
State Executive Branch		
State Judicial Branch		

CHAPTER REVIEW

Foldables Follow-Up Activity

Organize students into small groups. Students should use their completed foldables to think about how each state government's branch limits the power of the others. Remind students that state and national government branches operate much the same way. Using colored pencils or markers, students should create a diagram displaying specific examples of this information. Students should use visual elements such as connecting lines or arrows to demonstrate relationships.

Alternative Activities for Chapter 12

EVALUATING

Have students create a foldable about the legislative branches of any three states. They should first research to find the makeup of each state legislature. Students should include the size, name, qualifications for members, and so on, and write these facts on their foldables. They should then research problems currently facing each state's legislature, and write these on their foldables as well. Ask for volunteers to share the information they found.

State Legislatures	Makeup	Problems
Georgia		
Nebraska		
Vermont		

Governors	Accomplishments	Compare
Name: State:		
Name: State:		
Name: State:		

COMPARING

Instruct students to research to find the names of three governors, past or present. They should then use their table foldables to record information on each governor's accomplishments. Advise students to use the last column of their foldables to compare the governors they have selected. They can include similarities, differences, or both. Have students choose one of their governors to present to the class in a short oral report.

Student Study Tip

Give students the following tips on giving oral presentations. First, students should introduce their audience to their topic. Next, they should focus on the content of their presentation. This is where they should spend the most time. Remind them to speak clearly and to avoid phrases such as *um* and *like*. If students use visual aids, they should make sure the visual aids reinforce or illustrate a point. Students should conclude their presentation by giving a summary of the main points they covered.

Chapter 12

FOLDABLES

Local Government

CHAPTER SUMMARY

The U.S. Constitution does not mention local governments. They are created by, and are dependent upon, the state. State constitutions usually establish the powers and duties of local governments. There are several kinds of local governments, including city, county, town, township, and village. A city charter usually creates one of three forms of government: the mayor-council form, the council-manager form, or the commission form. County governments act as legislatures, decide on budgets, levy taxes, and plan for the health and safety of county residents. A board of three to five elected commissioners governs most counties. Just as many states are divided into counties, counties are divided into smaller political units such as towns or townships. Here, the everyday needs of American citizens are addressed.

CHAPTER PREVIEW

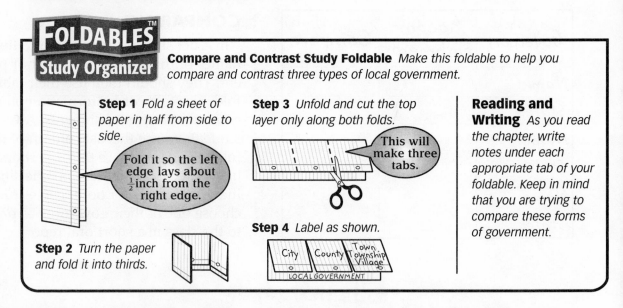

FOLDABLES™ Study Organizer

Compare and Contrast Study Foldable *Make this foldable to help you compare and contrast three types of local government.*

Step 1 *Fold a sheet of paper in half from side to side.*

Fold it so the left edge lays about ½ inch from the right edge.

Step 2 *Turn the paper and fold it into thirds.*

Step 3 *Unfold and cut the top layer only along both folds.*

This will make three tabs.

Step 4 *Label as shown.*

City | County | Town Township Village

LOCAL GOVERNMENT

Reading and Writing *As you read the chapter, write notes under each appropriate tab of your foldable. Keep in mind that you are trying to compare these forms of government.*

CHAPTER REVIEW

Foldables Follow-Up Activity

Have students use their foldable as the starting point for a research paper on a form of local government of their choosing. Instruct them to contact this unit of government via its offices or the Internet Web site. Research papers should include the government's structure and the services it provides. Encourage students to help each other find sources of information. Ensure that students compile the information they find in a well-organized report.

Alternative Activities for Chapter 13

EXPLAINING

Have students create this foldable to explain the three different forms of city government. Suggest to students that they keep their explanations simple and concise. Then have students use library or Internet resources to find a city that uses each form of city government. Encourage them to discuss as a class the pros and cons of each form. Make sure they know which form their city, or the city closest to them, utilizes.

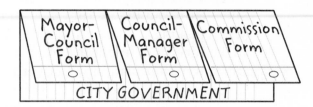

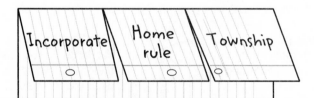

DEFINING

Ask students to choose three Key Terms from this chapter that they are most unfamiliar with. Students should define each term in their own words under the appropriate tab. Instruct students to write a sentence using each term as well. Then organize the class into pairs and have students quiz each other on the definitions. If their definitions vary, have them work together to construct the most precise definition possible.

Student Study Tip

To help students take notes on the information presented in their textbooks, have them convert each main head in the section into a question. Students should use words such as *who, what, when, where* or *why* to form their questions. For example, students might ask themselves: What is a metropolitan area? After students have created their questions, they should read the section to find the answers.

Chapter 13 FOLDABLES

Dealing With Community Issues

CHAPTER SUMMARY

Local governments and their planning commissions must consider short-term and long-term plans and evaluate priorities and resources when making public policy. After doing this, a planning commission makes decisions about the community's future and writes a document called a master plan. If the government accepts this plan, it becomes public policy. Local school leaders face several challenges such as funding issues, low test scores, high dropout rates, and crime and violence on school property. Community leaders must also concern themselves with social programs and protecting the environment.

CHAPTER PREVIEW

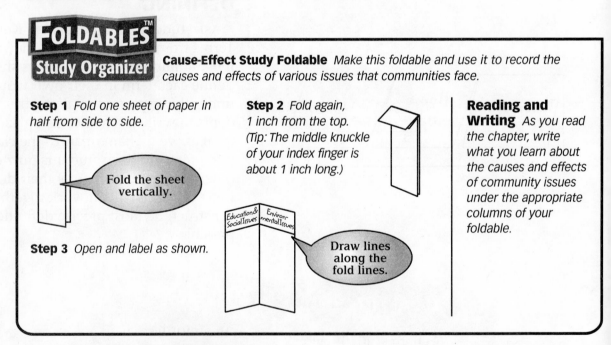

FOLDABLES™
Study Organizer

Cause-Effect Study Foldable *Make this foldable and use it to record the causes and effects of various issues that communities face.*

Step 1 *Fold one sheet of paper in half from side to side.*

Fold the sheet vertically.

Step 2 *Fold again, 1 inch from the top. (Tip: The middle knuckle of your index finger is about 1 inch long.)*

Step 3 *Open and label as shown.*

Education & Social Issues   Environmental Issues

Draw lines along the fold lines.

Reading and Writing *As you read the chapter, write what you learn about the causes and effects of community issues under the appropriate columns of your foldable.*

CHAPTER REVIEW

Foldables Follow-Up Activity

Organize the class into small groups and have them create posters titled *Dealing With Community Issues*. Instruct students to clip headlines, articles, and photos from local newspapers that deal with education, social, and environmental issues. Have them tape or paste these items on a poster board and then explain to the rest of the class how their community is handling the issues. Display the posters around the classroom.

Alternative Activities for Chapter 14

IDENTIFYING

A master plan for a community must take into account the community's priorities and the resources available to it. Have students complete this foldable by listing different priorities and resources that might be considered in their communities. Lead a class discussion about how difficult these decisions might be for community leaders. Ask why they think some residents might have different priorities than others.

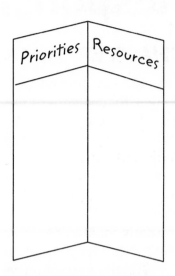

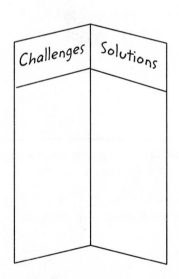

PROBLEM SOLVING

Have students create a foldable that lists several challenges to schools and teachers in one column and possible solutions in the other. After each student has created a foldable, organize students into small groups to research how several communities solved one of these challenges. Ask for groups to share the information they find, and to point out if they think their solution would also have worked and why.

Student Study Tip

Remind students to practice good study habits. Encourage them to study difficult topics first when they are fresh, choose a place to study where distractions are minimal, and avoid lengthy study sessions in which exhaustion impedes learning. They should also take breaks frequently to help remain focused.

Chapter 14 FOLDABLES

Legal Rights and Responsibilities

CHAPTER SUMMARY

The Constitution and the Bill of Rights contain important provisions, or laws, that safeguard the rights of Americans. Laws are sets of rules that allow people to live together peacefully in society. A major purpose of laws is to keep the peace and prevent violent acts. They set punishments and rules for resolving disputes. Early laws like the Code of Hammurabi, the Ten Commandments, Roman law, and English law have influenced our laws today. In addition to criminal law, there are other less well-known kinds of law, including civil law, public law, and international law. The American legal system offers protection to its citizens, including those who are accused of crimes. In return, the system gives Americans certain responsibilities such as serving on juries. Other responsibilities include obeying laws and cooperating with law enforcement officials.

CHAPTER PREVIEW

Summarizing Information Study Foldable *Make this foldable journal about our legal rights and responsibilities, and use it as a study guide.*

Step 1 *Fold a sheet of paper in half from top to bottom.*

Step 2 *Fold it in half again from side to side and label as shown.*

Reading and Writing *As you read the chapter, use your "law journal" to write what you learn about the types of laws, their sources, and their impact on Americans.*

CHAPTER REVIEW

Foldables Follow-Up Activity

After students have completed their "law journal" foldables, have them use the information to create quizzes for a classmate. Students should create a matching quiz of at least 10 questions. Then ask students to trade quizzes with a classmate and see how many types of laws they can match correctly. Ask for several volunteers to write their quizzes on the board for everyone to try. Encourage students to write any information they do not know in their notebooks so they can study it later.

Alternative Activities for Chapter 15

EXPLAINING

Have students create and use this foldable for all Key Terms in the chapter. As students read through the chapter, instruct them to record the Key Terms and their definitions in their *Journal of Key Terms*. Students should also use the term in a sentence and be able to explain why the term is significant. Ask several students to read several of their definitions aloud and have the rest of the class identify the correct term.

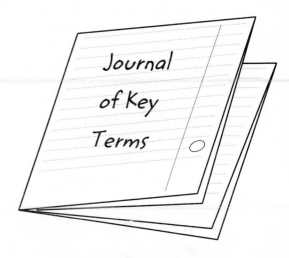

SUMMARIZING

Have students create a foldable that summarizes the rights of the accused. Tell them to include a brief explanation and background of the Fourth, Fifth, Sixth, and Eighth Amendments. Then students should research to find specific court cases such as *Miranda* v. *Arizona* that illustrate when these constitutional rights were protected.

Student Study Tip

Point out that the first word in a question signals the task that is required to successfully answer the question. Words such as *List* or *Identify* emphasize information collection. Other words require a description such as *Describe* or *Explain*. Still others ask students to compare information. Ask students to look through the questions in Chapter 15 and discuss the kinds of answers required.

Chapter 15 **FOLDABLES**

Civil and Criminal Law

CHAPTER SUMMARY

Both civil and criminal cases must follow a legal process or procedure. Civil law cases include disputes over rights, property, or agreements. Criminal cases are divided into two main groups—felonies and misdemeanors. A strict procedure, from arrest to the verdict and sentencing, determines how criminal cases are resolved. These cases end in either the acquittal of a defendant or the sentencing of a defendant who has been found guilty. Criminal cases that involve young people, or juveniles, follow a standard procedure that is different from the adult system. Juvenile courts emphasize rehabilitating, or correcting the behavior of, the offenders.

CHAPTER PREVIEW

FOLDABLES™
Study Organizer

Organizing Information Study Foldable *Make the following foldable to help you organize what you learn about civil and criminal law.*

Step 1 *Fold a sheet of paper into thirds from top to bottom.*

This forms three rows.

Step 2 *Open the paper and refold it into thirds from side to side.*

Fold it into thirds.
This forms three columns.

Reading and Writing *As you read the chapter, record what you learn about criminal and civil cases and court procedures in the appropriate spaces on your foldable table.*

Step 3 *Unfold, turn the paper, and draw lines along the folds.*

Step 4 *Label your table as shown.*

	Types of Cases	Court Procedures
Civil Law		
Criminal Law		

CHAPTER REVIEW

Foldables Follow-Up Activity

Direct students to www.ojp.usdoj.gov/bjs, which is the U.S. Department of Justice Web site for the Bureau of Justice Statistics. Explain that this Web site includes a wide range of information from sentencing statistics to expenditures of the justice system. Instruct students to choose one area and then compile a list of 10 statistics about the justice system. Ask for volunteers to read the statistics they chose from their lists.

Alternative Activities for Chapter 16

CATEGORIZING

Have students create this foldable to learn about the different kinds of crimes and the penalties for these crimes. Instruct students to read Section 2 and find examples of crimes against people and crimes against property to fill in their foldables. Then students should write the penalties for these crimes. Remind students that often judges have the power to choose from many different penalties in the sentencing process.

	Crimes Against People	Crimes Against Property
Examples of Crime		
Penalties for Crime		

	Neglect Cases	Delinquency Cases
Case Examples		
Rehabilitation Methods		

ORGANIZING

Juvenile courts generally handle neglect and delinquency cases. Have students create this foldable to understand the differences between these two cases. Students should write two to three examples of both neglect and delinquency cases and then write rehabilitation methods for each. When students have completed their foldables, lead a class discussion about the juvenile system and why rehabilitation is important for young people.

Student Study Tip

As students are studying each chapter, have them write important facts on index cards: Key Terms, dates, important people, court cases, and so on. Remind students to review their cards throughout the study of the chapter. Students may want to quiz each other using their index cards before taking the chapter test.

Chapter 16 FOLDABLES

Citizenship and the Internet

CHAPTER SUMMARY

Today millions of people have access to computers, the Internet, and the World Wide Web, all of which can be used by Americans to increase their knowledge of political and social issues. The Internet is increasing opportunities for citizens to participate in democracy because information about current events is readily available. There are many Web sites including those by the U.S. government, special-interest groups, candidates running for political office, and research and educational institutes. Computer access varies by race and family income level. The wealthiest families are much more likely to have computer access than families at lower income levels, according to the U.S. Census Bureau. The Internet also presents challenges such as limits on free speech, taxation of e-commerce, and protection of intellectual property.

CHAPTER PREVIEW

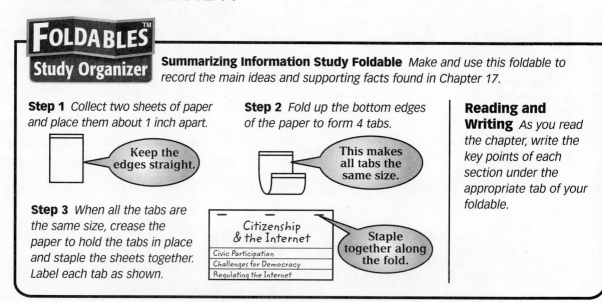

FOLDABLES™ Study Organizer

Summarizing Information Study Foldable *Make and use this foldable to record the main ideas and supporting facts found in Chapter 17.*

Step 1 *Collect two sheets of paper and place them about 1 inch apart.*

Keep the edges straight.

Step 2 *Fold up the bottom edges of the paper to form 4 tabs.*

This makes all tabs the same size.

Reading and Writing *As you read the chapter, write the key points of each section under the appropriate tab of your foldable.*

Step 3 *When all the tabs are the same size, crease the paper to hold the tabs in place and staple the sheets together. Label each tab as shown.*

Citizenship & the Internet
Civic Participation
Challenges for Democracy
Regulating the Internet

Staple together along the fold.

CHAPTER REVIEW

Foldables Follow-Up Activity

After students have created their foldables, organize the class into small groups. Have groups choose a government Web site to evaluate. Students should make a list of what they like about the site and what they think could be improved. Ask groups to sketch a new design for the site and then share with the class how they would redesign the site they chose.

Alternative Activities for Chapter 17

DESCRIBING

Organize students into three groups to create this foldable. Students should use library or Internet resources to research the history of the Internet. Assign each group a different question on their foldables. Have one group find *when* the Internet was created, the second find *where* it was created, and the third find *how* the Internet was created. Then have each group share their findings so students can complete their foldables.

History of
the Internet
When?
Where?
How?

Regulating
the Internet
Intellectual Property
Taxing E-Commerce
Internet at School

PREDICTING CONSEQUENCES

Students should work with a partner to find information in the library or on the Internet about *intellectual property, taxing e-commerce,* and the *Internet at school.* They should write down at least one source or Web site for each issue under the appropriate tabs of their foldables. Ask for volunteers to share the sources they found and discuss how possible Internet regulations might affect them.

Student Study Tip

Students with decoding problems may skip unfamiliar words. Often, however, they can comprehend words based on the context. When assigning a reading, ask students to write unfamiliar words in their notes. Then encourage students to deduce the meaning of each word based on the content. If they are still unsure of the meanings, have them look up the words in a dictionary.

Chapter 17 FOLDABLES

What Is Economics?

CHAPTER SUMMARY

Economics is the study of how individuals and societies make choices about ways to use scarce resources to fulfill their needs and wants. Economists define needs as those things that are necessary for survival. Wants are those things we desire but are not needed to survive. In making economic decisions, individuals face trade-offs among alternatives. A wise individual will consider opportunity costs to an action and perform a cost-benefit analysis to determine the best course of action. In a market economy, people and businesses act in their own best interests to answer the questions of *what, how,* and *for whom.* The study of economics helps people make informed decisions.

CHAPTER PREVIEW

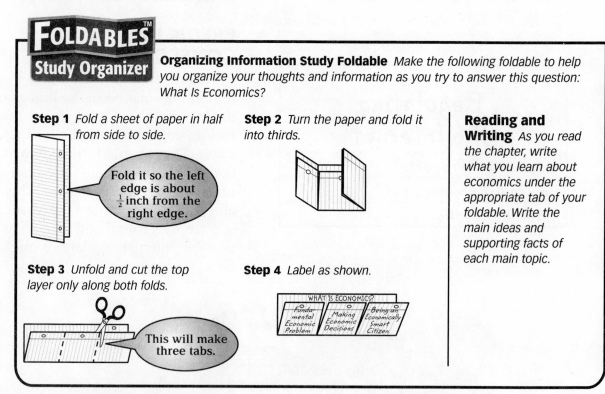

FOLDABLES™
Study Organizer

Organizing Information Study Foldable *Make the following foldable to help you organize your thoughts and information as you try to answer this question: What Is Economics?*

Step 1 *Fold a sheet of paper in half from side to side.*

Fold it so the left edge is about $\frac{1}{2}$ inch from the right edge.

Step 2 *Turn the paper and fold it into thirds.*

Step 3 *Unfold and cut the top layer only along both folds.*

This will make three tabs.

Step 4 *Label as shown.*

WHAT IS ECONOMICS?
Fundamental Economic Problem | Making Economic Decisions | Being an Economically Smart Citizen

Reading and Writing *As you read the chapter, write what you learn about economics under the appropriate tab of your foldable. Write the main ideas and supporting facts of each main topic.*

CHAPTER REVIEW

Foldables Follow-Up Activity

After students have completed their foldables, ask students to write a one-page story about a fictitious trip to a mall or department store. Have students try to use as many Key Terms from Chapter 18 as they can. Remind students that the terms apply to individuals and businesses. Encourage students to illustrate their stories.

Alternative Activities for Chapter 18

DECISION MAKING

Have students create this foldable to help them learn the importance of making an economic decision. Ask students to think of a particular example to answer the questions that all societies and economies face—*what, how,* and *for whom.* They should write the answers to these questions for their particular examples under the appropriate tabs. Have volunteers share their foldables with a partner.

ECONOMIC CHOICES

What to Produce | How to Produce | For Whom to Produce

ECONOMIC CONSIDERATIONS

Fixed Costs | Variable Costs | Marginal Costs

DRAWING INFERENCES

Businesses must consider many factors in choosing the best way to make a profit. Have students complete this foldable to learn about three of these factors—*fixed costs, variable costs,* and *marginal costs.* Students should explain each term and also provide examples under the appropriate tabs of their foldables. Lead a class discussion about how these costs might relate to the costs that are passed on to the consumer.

Student Study Tip

To help students with reading comprehension, point out the importance of headings and subheadings for understanding the structure and subject of each section and chapter. Once students are aware of the headings, this will help them categorize information as they read the material. It will also help them take well-organized notes.

The American Economy

CHAPTER SUMMARY

Four factors of production are required to produce goods and services—natural resources, labor, capital, and entrepreneurs. One measure of an economy's size is its Gross Domestic Product (GDP). This is the total value, in dollars, of all the final goods and services produced in a country during a single year. Productivity relates to the efficient use of resources. The United States has a free enterprise, or capitalist, system. Important characteristics include markets, economic freedom, competition, private property rights, the profit motive, and voluntary exchange. Consumers have rights and responsibilities, and citizens should be aware of these to make sound economic decisions.

CHAPTER PREVIEW

FOLDABLES™
Study Organizer

Summarizing Information Study Foldable *Make this foldable to help you organize and summarize what you learn about the American economy.*

Step 1 *Mark the midpoint of a side edge of one sheet of paper. Then fold the outside edges in to touch the midpoint.*

Step 2 *Fold the paper in half again from side to side.*

Reading and Writing *As you read the chapter, write information under each appropriate tab of your foldable. Be sure to summarize the information you find by writing only main ideas and supporting details on your foldable.*

Step 3 *Open the paper and cut along the inside fold lines to form four tabs.*

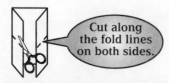

Cut along the fold lines on both sides.

Step 4 *Label as shown.*

Economic Resources | Circular Flow of Economic Activity
Characteristics of Capitalism | Economy & You

CHAPTER REVIEW

Foldables Follow-Up Activity

Organize students into groups of four. Each member of the group should ask one follow-up question to a main heading labeled on the front of their completed foldable. For example, a student might choose the heading *Economy & You*, and ask: "What is an example of a consumer responsibility?" The other group members should try to answer the follow-up question using the information on their foldables.

Alternative Activities for Chapter 19

ORGANIZING

Have students make and use this fold-able to organize information about the groups of economic decision makers involved in the circular flow of economic activity. Students should label their foldables as shown and then write as much information as they can under each tab of their foldables. On the back of their foldables, ask students to sketch their own economic flowchart to make sure they understand this concept.

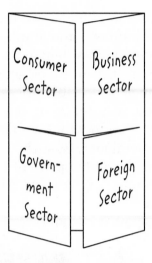

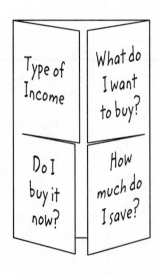

EVALUATING

Organize the class into groups of four and have each group complete a fold-able concerning their role as consumers. Present them with the following scenario. They have worked all summer and have earned $200. Now they must decide if they should spend the money, and if so, how they should spend the money. Each group should answer the questions on their foldables, and then present their decisions to the class with justification for their choices.

Student Study Tip

Remind students that their notes should be concise. Notes should briefly describe the main ideas and list supporting details. Students should use key words or phrases, rather than complete sentences or paragraphs, to help them remember specific information or concepts.

Chapter 19 FOLDABLES

Demand

CHAPTER SUMMARY

Demand has a specific meaning in economics. It refers to the desire, willingness, and ability to buy a good or service. Demand can be summarized in a demand schedule, which is a table that lists the various quantities of a product or service that someone is willing to buy over a range of possible prices. Demand can also be shown graphically in a downward-sloping demand curve. A demand curve shows the amount of a product that would be bought at all possible prices in the market. Several factors, such as changes in consumer incomes, tastes, expectations, and the price of related goods, can cause demand to either increase or decrease. All products and services are not affected by these factors in the same way, however. Economists call this phenomenon demand elasticity.

CHAPTER PREVIEW

Organizing Information Study Foldable *Make the following foldable to help you organize information about demand in a market economy.*

Step 1 *Fold a sheet of paper into thirds from top to bottom.*

Step 2 *Turn the paper horizontally, unfold, and label the three columns as shown.*

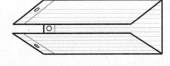

Reading and Writing *As you read the chapter, record your thoughts and the information you learn about demand in a market economy in the appropriate columns of your foldable.*

CHAPTER REVIEW

Foldables Follow-Up Activity

Once students have completed their foldables, they will have a study guide for the chapter. Have students use their completed foldables to prepare a one-page chapter test for a classmate to complete. Their tests should include 10 to 15 different types of questions. Questions may include short answer and essay questions, multiple-choice questions, true/false statements, and fill-in-the-blank statements. Students should also prepare answer keys for their tests and then exchange their tests with a classmate. Have students return the completed tests to the author for grading.

Alternative Activities for Chapter 20

IDENTIFYING

Students should label their foldables as shown. They should first identify the law of demand. They should then define *elastic demand* and *inelastic demand* and also give examples. Students should use examples of goods and services that are not in the textbook. Ask for volunteers to read their examples aloud and have the rest of the class identify whether demand is elastic or inelastic.

○ Law of Demand	○ Elastic Demand	○ Inelastic Demand

○ Milk	○ Video game	○ Sandals

DRAWING CONCLUSIONS

Have students write three products that they have purchased in the last year on their foldables. Then have them write the purchase price for each item and the date the item was purchased. Students should then find recent articles or advertisements about the products. Have them compare and analyze any change in price. They should use terms from the chapter such as *market demand* to explain these changes.

Student Study Tip

Information from the Internet is useful to students, but it should be reviewed critically. As students read material on the Internet, remind them to think of the author's biases. Students should try to identify the author's purpose for writing the information and how the author sometimes tries to influence the reader's opinion of the subject matter.

Chapter 20 FOLDABLES

Supply

CHAPTER SUMMARY

Supply refers to the various quantities of a good or service that producers are willing to sell at all possible market prices. For almost any good or service, the higher the price, the larger the quantity that will be offered for sale. The law of supply is the principle that suppliers will normally offer more for sale at higher prices and less at lower prices. The law of supply can be illustrated on a supply curve. Several factors can cause supply to either increase or decrease, such as changes in the cost of resources, productivity, technology, and government policies. Supply and demand work together to determine market price. A supply curve can be combined with a demand curve to analyze the price adjustment process. Prices are signals in our economy that help business and consumers make decisions. Prices also help answer the basic economic questions—WHAT to produce, HOW to produce, and FOR WHOM to produce.

CHAPTER PREVIEW

Organizing Information Study Foldable *Make the following foldable to help you organize information about supply in a market economy.*

Step 1 *Fold a sheet of paper into thirds from top to bottom.*

Step 2 *Turn the paper horizontally, unfold, and label the three columns as shown.*

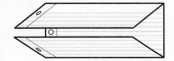

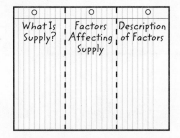

Reading and Writing *As you read the chapter, record your thoughts and the information you learn about supply in a market economy in the appropriate columns of your foldable.*

CHAPTER REVIEW

Foldables Follow-Up Activity

After students have completed their foldables, organize them into small groups. Instruct the groups to make posters illustrating the economic concept of supply. Suggest that they demonstrate the three subject fields of their foldables using definitions, drawings, headlines, and other visuals clipped from newspapers and magazines. Display the posters around the room. Then ask students to discuss what roles they specifically play in the marketplace.

Alternative Activities for Chapter 21

ORGANIZING

Have students label this foldable as shown. Students should define each term and provide an example for each one. For the last two terms, students should draw example graphs similar to those on page 463, but with different numbers and goods. If students have trouble graphing the supply numbers, invite a math teacher into the classroom to further explain the process.

Law of Supply	Supply Schedule	Supply Curve

EXPLAINING

Have students create this foldable to answer the economic questions of WHAT to produce, HOW to produce, and FOR WHOM to produce based on price. Students should act as business owners and choose a product or service to sell. They should determine the appropriate price by answering the economic questions on their foldables. Encourage students to repeat the process with a different product or service.

WHAT	HOW	FOR WHOM

Student Study Tip

Advise students that sequencing is helpful for organizing information. Suggest students number a very important fact or idea with the number 1, a lesser important idea with a 2, and so on while taking notes. When they go back over the material to study for a test, the most important information will be easier to find.

Chapter 21 FOLDABLES

Business and Labor

CHAPTER SUMMARY

In the United States, many important decisions are made by economic institutions. One of the institutions we encounter the most is the business organization. While businesses may vary in their organization, they all need a labor force. Often workers choose to organize themselves into a labor union. Labor unions seek increased wages and improved working conditions for their members. Businesses have responsibilities to their employees, consumers, stockholders, and the community. Businesses also have an obligation to pursue goals that benefit society as a whole, as well as themselves.

CHAPTER PREVIEW

FOLDABLES™
Study Organizer

Know-Want-Learn Study Foldable *Make this foldable to help you organize what you know, what you want to know, and what you learn about business and labor.*

Step 1 *Fold two sheets of paper in half from top to bottom. Cut the papers in half along the folds.*

Cut along the fold lines.

Step 2 *Fold each of the four papers in half from top to bottom.*

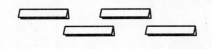

Step 3 *On each folded paper, make a cut 1 inch from the side on the top flap.*

1"

Cut 1 inch from the edge through the top flap only.

Step 4 *Place the folded papers one on top of the other. Staple the four sections together and label the top three tabs: Types of Businesses, Labor Unions, and Business in Our Economy.*

Staple here.

Types of Businesses

Reading and Writing *Before reading the chapter, write what you already know about the types of businesses, labor unions, and businesses in our economy under the tabs of your foldable. Also write one question you have on each tab. As you read, summarize what you learn under each tab.*

CHAPTER REVIEW

Foldables Follow-Up Activity

Organize the class into small groups to write one-page hypothetical business plans. The plans should include what good or service they will be selling, how their business will be organized, and how they will meet their responsibilities to employees, consumers, and the community. Groups should share their final plans with the class.

Alternative Activities for Chapter 22

ANALYZING

Have students research the history of three labor unions: the UAW, the USWA, and the AFL-CIO. Students should label their foldable tabs with these unions. Have them write what each acronym stands for and two facts about each organization on the back of the appropriate tab. Encourage students to find out if any of these labor unions are active in their area. If so, have them contact the unions to discover how many employees it represents and the services it offers.

Labor Unions Through History

Three Forms of Business Organizations

DESCRIBING

Students should label their foldable tabs with the three forms of business organizations and then write a brief description on the back of each tab. Then hold a class discussion on the advantages and disadvantages of each kind of organization. If you have extra time, have students cut out logos from local newspapers and affix them to the appropriate category.

Student Study Tip

Explain to students that summaries cover the main points succinctly. Remind students that they summarize information in order to write book reports, research for written or oral reports, and take notes on class lectures. To help students write summaries, have them begin by asking themselves, "What is this selection or discussion about?"

Chapter 22 FOLDABLES

Government and the Economy

CHAPTER SUMMARY

The federal government implements economic policies aimed at creating an economic environment favorable to growth and stability. The government encourages competition by enforcing antitrust laws and protects consumers with product safety laws. The government also creates fiscal policy to help control the business cycle. This fiscal policy most often includes changes in government spending or tax policies. To achieve a sensible fiscal policy, the government must be aware of a number of economic indices, including the unemployment rate, inflation, and the consumer price index. The federal government also tries to help individuals be economically successful. To accomplish this, the government encourages education, tries to reduce poverty, and uses a progressive income tax.

CHAPTER PREVIEW

FOLDABLES™
Study Organizer

Analyzing Information Study Foldable *Make this foldable to help you understand the role the government plays in maintaining economic stability, ways in which the economy is measured, and the impact these things have on your life.*

Step 1 *Mark the midpoint of the side edge of a sheet of paper.*

Draw a mark at the midpoint.

Step 2 *Fold the outside edges in to touch at the midpoint.*

Step 3 *Cut one of the large tabs in half to form two smaller tabs and label as shown.*

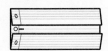

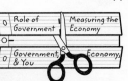

Role of Government | Measuring the Economy
Government & You | Economy,

Reading and Writing *As you read the chapter, take notes by writing information under each appropriate tab.*

CHAPTER REVIEW

Foldables Follow-Up Activity

Under the *Role of Government* tab, students should have noted information about federal regulatory agencies. Organize students into small groups and assign each group a different regulatory agency. Have groups research at the library or on the Internet to find two to three articles concerning their agency. Then ask one person from each group to share the importance of their agency, giving specific examples of what would happen if that agency did not exist.

Alternative Activities for Chapter 23

EXPLAINING

Organize students into pairs. Have them work together to create a foldable about government regulation of market activities. They should identify, define, and explain the three important areas that need government regulation—*natural monopolies, advertising and product labels*, and *product safety*. In the fourth section of their foldables, they should write *why* they think these areas require government regulation.

Natural Monopolies	Advertising & Product Labels
Product Safety	Why?

Why Prices Change	Stock Market Indexes
Stock Exchanges	Economy

DESCRIBING

Have students create this foldable to organize information about stocks and stock markets. Have students work in groups of three or four, and label their foldables as shown. Using the information in Section 2, they should write information under the appropriate tabs of their foldables. After students have finished filling out their foldables, ask them to find yesterday's stock market performance in the newspaper. Have them summarize the stock market results in one paragraph.

Student Study Tip

Let students know that when they take notes, they can use whatever style of note-taking works best for them. Different note taking styles include using formal and informal outlines, using diagrams, using charts or tables, drawing cause-and-effect charts, highlighting information using different colors of ink or highlighters, using abbreviations, and so on.

Chapter 23 FOLDABLES

Money and Banking

CHAPTER SUMMARY

The basis of the market economy is voluntary exchange. In the American economy, the exchange usually involves money in return for goods and services. Money also functions as a store of value, a measure of value, and part of a broader financial system. There are three types of financial institutions—commercial banks, savings and loan associations (S&Ls), and credit unions—that give people a safe place to deposit their money. The Federal Reserve serves as the government's bank. It controls monetary policy and regulates commercial banks in the United States. Banks provide services to consumers, such as savings and checking accounts, and they make a profit by lending money to consumers.

CHAPTER PREVIEW

FOLDABLES™
Study Organizer

Summarizing Information Study Foldable *Make this foldable and use it to record what you learn about money and banking.*

Step 1 *Collect two sheets of paper and place them about 1 inch apart.*

Keep the edges straight.

Step 2 *Fold up the bottom edges of the paper to form four tabs.*

This makes all tabs the same size.

Step 3 *When all the tabs are the same size, crease the paper to hold the tabs in place and staple the sheets together. Label each tab as shown.*

Staple together along the fold.

Money & Banking
What Is Money?
The Federal Reserve System
How Banks Operate

Reading and Writing *As you read, identify the key points of each section in the chapter and write these main ideas under the appropriate tabs of your foldable.*

CHAPTER REVIEW

Foldables Follow-Up Activity

After students have created their foldables, organize the class into small groups. Have students create flash cards with information from their foldables. Students may want to include pictures, diagrams, definitions, and facts on their flash cards. Encourage students to use colored pencils or markers to create their flash cards, and to use their flash cards as a study tool for the chapter test.

Alternative Activities for Chapter 24

ORGANIZING

Have students complete this foldable to help them understand the structure of the Federal Reserve System, known as the Fed. Students should label their foldables as shown, and describe each component under the appropriate tabs of their foldables. On the back of their foldables, have them list the location of the 12 district banks and identify the district bank closest to them. Have students sketch a rough map that shows the locations of all 12 district banks.

Structure of the Fed
Board of Governors
Advisory Councils
FOMC

Changes in Banking
The Great Depression
Savings and Loan Crisis
Gramm-Leach-Bliley Act

IDENTIFYING

Students should identify three changes that affected the banking industry and write these on their foldables. Under the appropriate tabs of their foldables, they should explain how each event affected banking. Then have students write a half-page newspaper article about one of the events. The article should explain what happened and what the impact was on the banking industry.

Student Study Tip

Explain to students that teachers and textbook writers often use signal words or phrases when lecturing or writing. Signal phrases such as "There are three reasons why...," "More importantly," and "A major development..." signal that main ideas are being expressed. Phrases such as "on the other hand" or "on the contrary" signal contrasting ideas. Students can take better notes if they recognize these signal words and phrases.

Chapter 24 FOLDABLES

Government Finances

CHAPTER SUMMARY

Every year, the federal government prepares a budget that accounts for trillions of dollars in revenues and expenditures. The income tax paid by individual Americans supplies nearly half of all the federal government's revenue. The federal government's largest expenditures include Social Security, national defense, and income security. State and local governments also have to prepare budgets every year. The main source of state government revenue is intergovernmental revenue, which is money that one level of government receives from another level. Elementary and secondary education is the largest single category of spending for local governments.

CHAPTER PREVIEW

Organizing Information Study Foldable *Make the following foldable to help you organize what you learn about financing our government.*

Step 1 *Collect two sheets of paper and place them about 1 inch apart.*

Keep the edges straight.

Step 2 *Fold up the bottom edges of the paper to form four tabs.*

This makes all tabs the same size.

Reading and Writing *As you read the chapter, use your foldable to write what you learn about the revenues and expenditures of governments in the United States under each appropriate tab.*

Step 3 *When all the tabs are the same size, crease the paper to hold the tabs in place and staple the sheets together. Label each tab as shown. Then cut the three lower tabs in half, forming six tabs.*

Staple together along the fold.

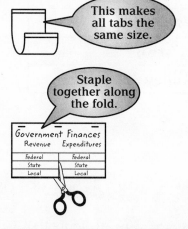

CHAPTER REVIEW

Foldables Follow-Up Activity

Students should use their completed foldables to discuss revenues and expenditures at the federal, state, and local government levels. Manage the discussion by calling out a specific type of revenue or expenditure. Then have students identify which level of government has that specific type of revenue or expenditure. Continue the activity until each student has had a chance to participate.

Alternative Activities for Chapter 25

EXPLAINING

Students should *not* cut the three lower tabs in half as shown in Step 3 to create this foldable. They should label the foldable as shown to define and explain the different forms of taxation in the U.S. today. Then organize students into small groups to research the forms of taxation in other countries. You may assign each group a different country or allow the groups to choose.

```
  ___        ___          ___
 Forms of Taxation

   Proportional
   Progressive
   Regressive
```

```
  ___        ___          ___
  Fiscal Policy

 In theory...
 In practice...
 Automatic Stabilizers
```

ANALYZING

Students should *not* cut the three lower tabs in half as shown in Step 3 to create this foldable. They should label the tabs as shown. Remind students that fiscal policy is the federal government's use of spending and taxation policies to affect overall business activity. Students should draw diagrams to illustrate what happens in different scenarios both in theory and in practice. They should then define *automatic stabilizers* and provide examples.

Student Study Tip

Before students answer the question about a map, chart, or graph, remind them to study the graphic carefully to understand what information is being presented and what is being asked in the question. Students should read the title, labels, keys, or axes to learn about the graphic's subject and note how the data is organized.

Chapter 25 FOLDABLES

Comparing Economic Systems

CHAPTER SUMMARY

International trade is one of the major forces in the world today. Nations can solve the problem of scarcity by trading with other nations. Countries sometimes institute trade barriers, such as tariffs or quotas to remedy situations where consumers are not buying domestic products. There are several types of economic systems, such as market economies, command economies, and mixed economies. Today many nations are making the transition from one type of economy to another and face severe challenges. However, developing nations receive financing through foreign aid and technical and economic assistance. The main reason for the transition from command economies to market-based systems is the success of market economies in the world.

CHAPTER PREVIEW

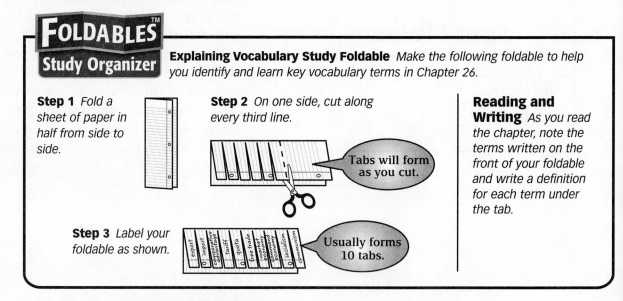

FOLDABLES™
Study Organizer

Explaining Vocabulary Study Foldable *Make the following foldable to help you identify and learn key vocabulary terms in Chapter 26.*

Step 1 *Fold a sheet of paper in half from side to side.*

Step 2 *On one side, cut along every third line.*

Tabs will form as you cut.

Step 3 *Label your foldable as shown.*

Usually forms 10 tabs.

Reading and Writing *As you read the chapter, note the terms written on the front of your foldable and write a definition for each term under the tab.*

CHAPTER REVIEW

Foldables Follow-Up Activity

Once students have created their foldables, have them write a series of journal entries or short newspaper articles using most of the terms on their foldables. If students have difficulty getting started, suggest they write a sentence for each term, and then tie the sentences together into a paragraph. They can then add specific details to make the paragraph into an informative newspaper article or journal entry. Ask for volunteers to read their articles or entries to the rest of the class.

Alternative Activities for Chapter 26

COMPARING

Have students choose 10 countries to write on their foldables. Students should research to find what kind of economic system each country has. They should write this information under each appropriate tab. Initiate a class discussion about why countries have different economic systems. Point out that many countries, such as Russia and China, are in transition from a command economy to a market economy, and have students explain why.

DESCRIBING

To create this foldable, in Step 2, students should cut along every ninth line of their sheet of paper to create three sections. Then students should label the three tabs with the different types of regional trade agreements as shown. Ask: What countries belong to each organization? What is the purpose of each organization? Students should write these answers under the appropriate tabs of their foldables.

Student Study Tip

Have students take notes after they have read long paragraphs in the section rather than at the end of the chapter. This helps them focus on important ideas and details and prevents them from losing track of the flow of information. Remind students that they should not spend a long time taking notes on the section. Students should read, think, write, and move on.

Chapter 26 **FOLDABLES**

Comparing Systems of Government

CHAPTER SUMMARY

There are different types of governments in different countries. Governments are often placed into two categories: those that are democratic and those that are authoritarian. In democratic regimes, the people rule. In authoritarian regimes, power is held by an individual or group that is not accountable to the people. Great Britain developed the parliamentary system of government. Most former British colonies—Australia, Canada, India, and so on—have patterned their own governments after Britain's. China's leaders, on the other hand, established a totalitarian government strictly controlled by the Communist Party. Recently, however, China has begun to allow some elements of free enterprise.

CHAPTER PREVIEW

Compare and Contrast Study Foldable *Make this foldable and use it to help you identify similarities and differences in governments around the world.*

Step 1 *Mark the midpoint of a side edge of one sheet of paper. Then fold the outside edges in to touch at the midpoint.*

Step 2 *Fold the paper in half from side to side.*

Step 4 *Label as shown.*

Step 3 *Open and cut along the inside fold lines to form four tabs.* Cut along the fold lines on both sides.

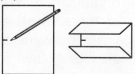

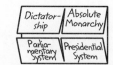

Dictator-ship	Absolute Monarchy
Parlia-mentary System	Presidential System

Reading and Writing *As you read the chapter, write information under each tab to help you compare and contrast different types of governments and the countries where they are in place.*

CHAPTER REVIEW

Foldables Follow-Up Activity

Organize students into pairs. Have students take turns asking their partner questions based on the information that is written on their foldables. Students should ask different kinds of questions, such as true/false or fill-in-the-blank, about the different types of governments. For every wrong answer, the student asking the question should ask a different type of question until the correct answer is given.

Alternative Activities for Chapter 27

ORGANIZING

Have students create and complete this foldable about Great Britain by labeling the foldable as shown. Students should write as much as they can under each tab so they get a firm grasp on how Great Britain's government works. After students have completed filling out their foldables, ask them to find one or two current newspaper or magazine articles about Great Britain and its government. Ask for volunteers to read a few paragraphs from their articles.

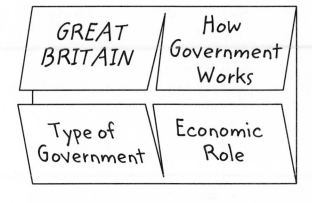

DESCRIBING

Have students complete this foldable about China by describing different aspects of the country, such as its history and structure of the government. After students have completed their foldables, ask students to research to find the most recent information about China. Ask students to write a one-page report summarizing what they find and to include a sketch of China's flag or a map of China.

Student Study Tip

Chapter 27 contains many facts. To help students remember what they have read, discuss some memorization techniques for them to use while studying. *Association*, or relating ideas to one another, is one way students can remember information. Students could also *visualize* as they read about different topics to form mental images. *Acronyms*, or invented combinations of letters, are also useful in remembering key words and ideas.

Chapter 27 FOLDABLES

An Interdependent World

CHAPTER SUMMARY

Global interdependence means that people and nations all over the world now depend upon one another for many goods and services. Since World War II, industrialized democracies have promoted free trade or the removal of trade barriers through the formation of regional associations. Internationalism is the idea that nations should cooperate to promote common aims, such as supporting economic development and fighting terrorism. They do this through membership in an organization made up of many nations, such as the United Nations (UN). The UN was established to maintain peace by guaranteeing the security of member nations. The UN is also concerned with issues such as human rights and the growth of democracy.

CHAPTER PREVIEW

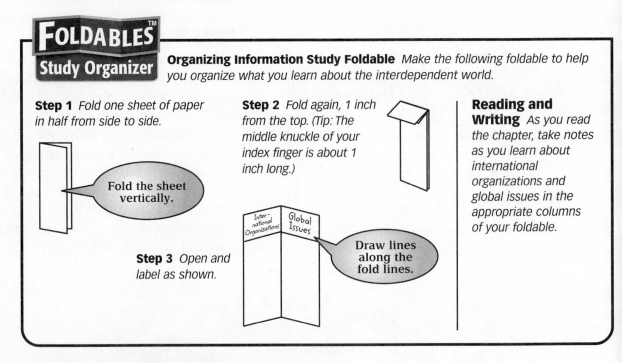

FOLDABLES™ Study Organizer

Organizing Information Study Foldable *Make the following foldable to help you organize what you learn about the interdependent world.*

Step 1 *Fold one sheet of paper in half from side to side.*

Fold the sheet vertically.

Step 2 *Fold again, 1 inch from the top. (Tip: The middle knuckle of your index finger is about 1 inch long.)*

Step 3 *Open and label as shown.*

International Organizations | Global Issues

Draw lines along the fold lines.

Reading and Writing *As you read the chapter, take notes as you learn about international organizations and global issues in the appropriate columns of your foldable.*

CHAPTER REVIEW

Foldables Follow-Up Activity

Organize students into small groups. Groups should create an imaginary television news program about international organizations and the global issues they deal with today. Groups should write interview questions for the secretary-general of the UN. A sample question is: "What are some of the recent activities of the UN?" Groups should also write a script of interview answers.

Alternative Activities for Chapter 28

DRAWING INFERENCES

Ask students to choose two UN agencies to write on their foldables. Students should research for information on the two agencies they chose, and then write this information under the appropriate heading on their foldables. Then lead a class discussion about UN agencies. Say an agency's name aloud, and ask students to call out what they think that agency might do based on its name. Ask students to share key points about the agencies they chose.

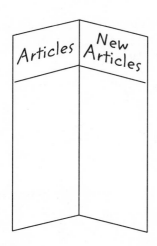

EVALUATING

Students should create this foldable about human rights by labeling their foldables as shown. In the left column, students will list several articles from the Universal Declaration of Human Rights and also write what each article protects. In the right column, students should list additional articles that they think should be added to the document.

Student Study Tip

Advise students that there are several words commonly found in essay test questions. Once students are familiar with some of these words, they will learn to answer the questions the best way possible. For example, with the word *analyze*, students should break the question into separate parts and discuss, examine, or interpret each part. For the word *evaluate*, students should consider the options, cite an opinion, and provide evidence to support the evaluation.

Chapter 28 FOLDABLES